ILLUSIONS

Illustrating Life Lessons Using Simple Illusions & Other Neat Stuff

---

David and Teesha Laflin
www.davidandteesha.com

ILLUSIONS
Copyright © 2010 by David and Teesha Laflin

ISBN: 978-0-692-00120-2

Table of Contents

Acknowledgments

Duane and Mary Laflin

>Thank you so much, Dad and Mom, for introducing us to the art of illusion. Thanks for teaching us, instructing us, guiding us, and helping us in so many ways. Much more importantly, thank you for setting an example that is worthy of being followed in both your marriage and in your relationship with Jesus.

Rebecca Lock

>You are an awesome photographer and a great big sister!

The Lock Kids

>Thanks for volunteering, you were all such a big help.

Shelly Stumpf

>Thank you for taking the time to read through and edit this book. You are an incredible Aunt and an inspiration to us both.

Preface

For more than seven years we have had the privilege of sharing the message of Jesus Christ around the world through the art of illusion. Illusions are an amazing tool for ministry, and we are very grateful for the opportunity to share some lessons with you in this book. Some of the effects you will master in moments. Others will take some time and practice. This book may even be a stepping stone for you toward learning much more about illusions. No matter what your goals are, there are a few things that are very important to remember when using illusions in ministry.

1. Explain that what you do is not real magic.

Most people understand this, but it is still very important to reassure your audience. All you really need to do is make a simple statement to the effect of: "Everything I do is just an illusion. God does miracles, I do tricks. But the truth behind each lesson is no illusion, and that's what I hope you remember!"

2. Practice!

It is extremely important for your message to be clear. The reality is that if you are unsure of yourself in your performance you will probably be so concerned about making sure you do the trick right that the message suffers. Practice to the point that you are confident in what you are doing, and then you can place your main focus on the message. There may still be times you mess up in a live performance. That's ok; simply use it as a learning experience and you will do better the next time!

3. Do not immediately repeat the same trick.

If you do a good job performing your trick, a common response will be: "Wow- do that again!" This is always very tempting because it feels so great to get that kind of response. But, if you do choose to immediately repeat the trick your audience will now be aware of what to watch for and much more likely to catch you. In fact, the second time through they are even likely to stop you in the middle of what you are doing to try and make you show them something more closely, "open your other hand", or let them examine something. One thing is certain; you are almost guaranteed to not get as good of a response when you repeat a trick immediately. The element of surprise is simply not the same. Instead, maybe have a different trick ready. This does not mean you can never do the trick again, just give it some time (a few days or weeks) so it will be special again!

4. Keep the secrets.

One of our favorite things about using illusions to communicate a message is the simple fact that people do try to figure out the trick! If they cannot figure it out, they will be likely to continue to think about it. And, when they think about the trick they will also be reminded of the message you shared! The amazement of the illusions adds to effectiveness of the message! If, on the other hand, you tell how the trick is done then two big problems occur. First, you can never again perform that trick for the same audience because they already know how it works! Second, and more importantly, the effectiveness of the message is lost. If you tell how the trick works then people will be more interested in going and sharing their newfound knowledge with others than they will be in remembering your message.

Introduction

As we finally boarded the plane for Bolivia we found our seats and took a huge sigh of relief. Several times previously we had traveled to other countries, but never had it been so difficult. But now, the worst was behind us and we were ready to embark on this new adventure and have some fun. Or, so we thought. The truth was that although we did have an amazing adventure ahead of us, the most difficult struggles had yet to begin.

The planning for this trip had begun like so many others. A team of 12 individuals was selected. Each one of us with different strengths and weaknesses that would hopefully mend together for greatness! The members of the team were from all across the United States, so for six months leading up to the trip we did our best to communicate across the distance and make the best possible preparations for the trip and the ministry we would be sharing there. With less than one month to departure, the first major obstacle arose. The airline we were scheduled to travel on called to let us know that our flight from Miami to La Paz, Bolivia had been cancelled. This created an extra difficulty for us because each member of the team had already also booked domestic tickets from their city to Miami. The plan was for each of us to arrive in Miami on separate flights, meet in the airport, and then travel together to Bolivia.

After much hard work and a lot of prayer, we were able to reschedule our flight to La Paz. We all decided to make the best of it and still fly to Miami on our previously scheduled domestic flights- two days early of our new flight to Bolivia. At least this would give us some extra time for team building and to review our plans.

Two days after arriving in Miami, we all returned to the airport for the trip to Bolivia. We were ready, but once again the airline was not. The flight was delayed. At first the delay was just an hour. Then two hours. Then four, then ten, then sixteen. Everyone stayed in great spirits all things considered. But, of course, 16 hours of playing games on the floor in the airport can start to drag on! All of us were relieved to finally be on the plane and moving down the runway. We were finally on our way!

We stood by the baggage carousel in La Paz, Bolivia waiting for our luggage to arrive. Through careful planning, each person on our team had packed one personal bag and one bag full of items for ministry. We were ready to gather the bags with our illusions, object lessons, puppets, crafts, donation items, and all of the other essentials we had careful been coordinating over the last six months. We stood patiently ready to retrieve our bags and get to work. Slowly the minutes passed, and no bags arrived. We continued to wait and pray for our bags. When our first two bags finally arrived we breathed one more sigh of relief. But, we soon discovered that those first two bags were also our last two bags. It turns out that all of our careful planning was for naught. The rest of the bags, filled with both our ministry tools and our clothes, were still in the airport in Miami. Our hopes did rise a bit when we were promised our bags would arrive the next day. That promise was never fulfilled. In fact, we never did see our bags again until we returned home from Bolivia.

Through all of this, many challenges arose. How could we possibly be effective here without our carefully crafted plan? Of course, in the end, God was in control. The reality of Psalms 19:21 became very real to us. This verse says "Many are the plans in a man's heart, but it is the Lord's purpose that prevails (NIV)." We were amazed to see how He took our agenda and set it aside so that we could experience something much greater.

One of the answers to the challenges we faced turned out to be much of what lies ahead in this book. The theme "Illusions You Can Make" was definitely put into practice there on the mission field. We had learned and even taught many of these illusions and effects over the years, but we had never tried to conduct an entire week of VBS using them as our primary teaching tools. Our creativeness was put to the test, and the team responded in grand fashion! The team came up with new crafts, games, and even made their own puppets. And everyday we shared the love of Jesus Christ with the people in Bolivia by using many of these illusions. God surprised us with how he was able to take these simple items and do incredible things. In 1 Corinthians 1:26-28 is a place in the Bible where God's desire to use that which the world views to be small to accomplish his big purposes is clearly explained.

> "Remember, brothers and sisters, that few of you were wise in the world's eyes, or powerful, or wealthy when God called you. Instead, God deliberately chose things the world considers foolish in order to shame those who think they are wise. And he chose those who are powerless to shame those who are powerful. God chose things despised by the world, things counted as nothing at all, and used them to make what the world considers important become nothing. (New Living Translation)"

How awesome to know that God can use each of us, even when the world might look down on us and think we have little to offer. He can take the smallest things of this world, which at first glance seem like nothing, and use them for His greatness! We hope and pray that you will enjoy the simplicity of these effects, but more importantly, the incredible messages they help to communicate. And, above all else, to God be the glory- great things *He* has done.

Chapter One
What God Wants

Could the God who created this universe and everything in it really want something else? Yes! What He wants – is you!

Verse: Luke 10:38-42 (New Living Translation)

As Jesus and the disciples continued on their way to Jerusalem, they came to a certain village where a woman named Martha welcomed them into her home. Her sister, Mary, sat at the Lord's feet, listening to what he taught. But Martha was distracted by the big dinner she was preparing. She came to Jesus and said, "Lord, doesn't it seem unfair to you that my sister just sits here while I do all the work? Tell her to come and help me."

But the Lord said to her, "My dear Martha, you are worried and upset over all these details! There is only one thing worth being concerned about. Mary has discovered it, and it will not be taken away from her."

Materials Needed:

(6) Pieces of card stock or poster board
(1) Mirror
(1) Marker
(1) Clip or Clothes Pin
Duct Tape

Concept:

Six separate cards are displayed. On the back of one is a representation of what God wants. An audience member selects a number between one and six. When the selected card is turned around, it is shown to have a mirror on it. What God really wants- is you!

13

How to do it:

No matter what number the volunteer selects, the end result will always be the same card. This card should be placed in the third position from the audience's left when all six cards are displayed (See Figure 1 - the third card is marked with a clip). If the number selected is one, simply spell out O-N-E to land on the third card. The same is true for two (T-W-O) and six (S-I-X). If the number is three, count 1-2-3. For the number four, begin counting from the right side. And for five, spell out F-I-V-E from the right side. When you arrive at the third card, mark it as the selected card. Reveal the other five cards first to show what was not chosen. Then, reveal the mirror last (See Figure 2).

Figure 1

Figure 2

Presentation:

Have you ever wondered if there was anything that God wants? If you think about it, God made this universe and everything in it- what else could He possibly want? The truth is that there is something God wants. Today we are going to see if we can find out what it is that God desires.

I have six separate cards. Behind one of them is something to help us think about this thing that God wants. To do this I am going to need a volunteer (choose your volunteer). I want you to nice and loudly name a number between one and six (we'll say they pick five). To make sure we are absolutely clear on this number, let's spell it out together F-I-V-E.

We will come back to that card in just a moment, but first let's look at these other things we are missing out on. Behind this picture it says Go To Church. Is that it? Is that what God wants the most? No, that is not it. Going to church is something God wants us to do, but the truth is there are people that go to church without really giving God that which He wants most.

The next card says Give Money. That is not it either. Giving money is important, but not the most important thing. How about this one here- Don't Have Fun. Is that it? Of course

15

not! Some people think that God is all about rules and does not want you to have fun, but that is not it either.

Next we have Dress To Impress. That must be it right? We always dress in our best clothes for church because God just wants us to dress up and look real nice, so He will like us! No, that is not it either.

How about this last one, Serve Others? Serving others is important, and it is something God does want. But, the thing God wants most is (turn around the selected card to reveal the mirror). YOU!!!

God desires to have a relationship with each and every one of you. In the verses we read today, Martha was busy trying to do all things she thought were most important, while Mary sat at the feet of Jesus listening to Him. If we just go through the motions and go to church, give money, and do all those other things because we are supposed to, but we fail to give Jesus ourselves, then we too have missed the most important thing!

Helpful Hints:

Do not put numbers on the front of the cards, or it will not make sense that you did not simply choose the number that was chosen by the audience. Instead, either leave them blank, or put the same design and color on all six pieces.

Also, stand stage left of the pictures (to the audience's right) when the audience member calls out the number. This way, it will not seem awkward if you start counting or spelling from the right (numbers four and five). Because we read left to right, it will also not be strange if you walk to the left side and begin counting or spelling (numbers one, two, three, and six).

Chapter Two
Give What You Can

God can take the ordinary and make it extraordinary!

Verse: Isaiah 43:18-19 (NIV)

Forget the former things; do not dwell on the past. See, I am doing a new thing! Now it springs up; do you not perceive it? I am making a way in the desert and streams in the wasteland.

Materials Needed:

(1) Fifty dollar bill (or any other amount)
(1) Blank piece of paper- cut the same size as the bill
Double-Stick tape

Concept:

A blank piece of paper is shown, folded into a small pack, and then opened back up to reveal it has changed to a $50 bill.

How to do it:

1.	Fold the $50 bill into a very small packet, as small as you can (figure #1).

2.	Place a piece of double stick tape on the back of the bill and stick it to the piece of paper, near one side; the paper should be pre-cut to be the same size as the bill (figure #2). When displayed to your audience, the bill will be hidden behind the packet (figure #3).

3.	Fold the piece of paper down into the same size packet as the bill (figure #4).

4. Under the cover of your hand turn this combined packet around so the bill is now facing your audience.

5. Slowly unfold the bill; it will appear that the piece of paper has now changed! (Figure #5a and #5b)

Figure #1

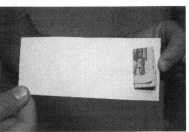

Figure #2

Figure #3

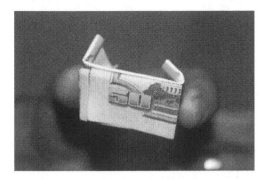

Figure #4

Figure #5a

Figure #5b

Presentation:

There are times in each of our lives in which we feel very ordinary, maybe like a plain piece of paper (hold up the plain paper). It is easy to think that there is nothing special about our lives. We might even look back at some of our failures in life; those times in which we tried our best but came up short, and begin to feel very small (begin folding the paper into a small packet) and unimportant. But, the amazing thing is (begin unfolding the pack to reveal the $50 bill) that God has given us a new hope.

In Isaiah 43 He says not to dwell on the past, but instead be ready for new things. God can make an amazing change in our life! He can take which was once thought to be ordinary and make it (hold up and display the $50 bill) extraordinary!

Helpful Hints:

Be extra careful to keep the $50 bill concealed when you are folding the ordinary piece of paper. When you unfold the $50 bill, keep it covered by your hands until it is unfolded enough that the white paper is now hidden behind.

You can obviously do this same trick with other denominations. Use it to change a $1 bill to a $5 bill. Or, you could change the blank piece of paper to a $1 bill and then "steal" the blank piece of paper off the back. This would enable you to hand out the bill for examination or give it away.

Chapter Three
Be Transformed!

Verse: Romans 12:2   (NIV)
      Do not conform any longer to the pattern of this world, but be transformed by the renewing of your mind. Then you will be able to test and approve what God's will is – His good, pleasing, and perfect will.

Materials Needed:
(2) Cups that you cannot see through (Figure #1)
(1) Duplicate cup filled with water
(1) Small sponge
Ice cubes

Figure #1

Concept:
      Water is poured into a cup, but when the cup is turned back over- ice comes out.

21

How to do it:

Begin by placing the sponge into the bottom of the empty cup. Add a few ice cubes on top of the sponge and you are ready to go (figure #2)!

As you pour water into the cup, the sponge at the bottom will absorb the water. The slower you pour, the more water it appears is going in. When the cup is turned back over, the water stays in, and the ice comes out!

Figure #2

Presentation:

There is a verse in the Bible that says "Do not be conformed to this world, but be transformed by the renewing of your mind." This is an important verse, but what exactly does that mean? It means that instead of being just like everybody else out there, we should be different. If we say we are followers of Jesus, our attitude and the way we act should be unlike the rest of the world.

How does this change happen? It begins when we make a decision to do all we can to live a life like Jesus. The more time we spend with God through reading our Bible, prayer, and spending time with other Christians who encourage us, the more we begin to understand how Jesus would truly wants us to act.

All of these things begin to pour into our lives (begin slowly pouring about an inch of water into the cup that has the ice and sponge in it - Figure #3) a knowledge and understanding of who Jesus wants us to be. Understanding, of course, involves our brain. You could call it "renewing your mind."

As we learn in our mind the way Jesus wants us to live, it should cause a transformation and change that becomes acted out in our lives. Hopefully, it will even be a significant enough change that others will see we are truly (Pour the ice back out into your hand - Figure #4) transformed!

Figure #3

Figure #4

Helpful Hints:

Be sure to practice ahead of time with the amount of water you can use with the cup and sponge you have selected. If you use too much water the sponge will not hold it.

Pour the water into the cup slowly. This creates the illusion of more water going in because the audience visually sees the water pouring for a longer length of time.

If you have problems with the ice cubes sticking to the sponge and not coming out, simply get both the sponge and ice cubes just a little bit wet before beginning.

Chapter Four
What Can YOU Accomplish?

Each one of us faces barriers in our lives that seem impossible to break through. When we face these barriers it is important to remember that with Jesus, there is always a way.

Verse: Philippians 4:13 (New Living Translation)
For I can do everything through Christ, who gives me strength.

Materials Needed:
(2) Rubber bands

Concept:
Two rubber bands are "locked" together illustrating the fact that we all face barriers that seem impossible to get through (Figure #1). Then, the rubber bands seemingly pass through one another right before the eyes of your audience.

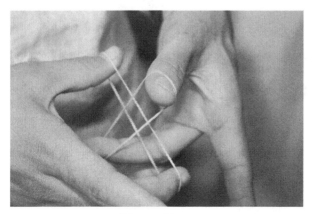

Figure #1

How to do it:

The secret to this illusion is simply changing the rubber band on one hand from the thumb and middle finger to the thumb and pointer finger. See the illustrations in figures #2 and #3 for more detail on this.

First, the rubber bands are interlocked (figure #1). They are then pulled against each other to illustrate the struggle against barriers (figure #2). As the rubber bands are returning from this stretched out position to their starting point, insert the pointer finger on your right hand into the rubber band beside the right thumb (figure #3). Now, begin to stretch the rubber band out between the pointer finger and the thumb, and allow the rubber band to release from your middle finger (figure #4). The bands should now be separated, but allow them to rest on top of each other for a moment, so the audience does not realize this has happened. Finally, rub the rubber bands together gently, and then slowly pull them apart (figure #5).

This does take a little practice, but it is definitely worth it. Good luck- and break through those barriers!

Figure #2

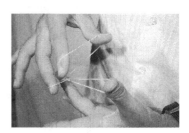

Figure #3

Figure #4   Figure #5

Presentation:

Have you ever been in a situation that seemed hopeless? All of us have probably found ourselves in a place where we faced some type of barrier that seemed impossible to break through.

Today these rubber bands are going to illustrate those barriers. When the rubber bands are "locked" together like this (interlock the bands between your thumb and middle fingers - figure #1), it would seem impossible for one to pass through the other. But, no matter what we face in life, it is important to remember that we can break through.

In Philippians 4:13 we are reminded that it does not matter what barrier is in our way, or how difficult the challenge we face is (begin to pull the rubber bands against each other as in figure #2 as you talk about these difficult challenges. Then switch your finger position as described above to release the rubber bands, but keep them close to each other so the audience does not yet know they are separated) we can do all things (now slowly show the rubber bands separated - Figure #4) through Christ who gives us strength!

Helpful Hints:

When you switch from your middle to finger to the pointer finger, this only needs to happen with one hand. In fact one hand does most, if not all, of the work. As this happens, stretch the rubber band directly over and on top of the other rubber band, so the audience does not immediately know they are separate. Blow on the rubber bands as you rub them together and slowly separate them. This will greatly enhance the illusion.

As you get better and better with this trick, you can add a twist to make it look even more impressive. Interlock the rubber bands, holding them between your thumb and first finger (instead of the middle finger as described above). All the work will be done with one hand only. If you are right-handed, your right hand will do the work, and if you are left-handed, the left hand does the work.

For a right-hander, hold your left hand palm up, right hand palm down with the rubber bands locked together. As you pull back with the right hand, curl the middle finger on your right hand over the top of your pointer finger, and momentarily transfer the rubber band to the middle finger. As this happens, you now continue (as above) and put your pointer finger in by your thumb, and stretch the rubber band in your right hand over the one in the left, releasing the rubber band. Now, instead of the rubber bands starting on one hand and finishing on another, they will start and finish on the same finger.

Chapter Five
The Right Choice

We do not always know the end result of the choices we make, but when we choose to live for Jesus, we can know we will experience His joy here on earth and eternity with Him in Heaven.

Verse: Joshua 24:15 (New Living Translation)
But if you refuse to serve the LORD, then choose today whom you will serve. Would you prefer the gods your ancestors served beyond the Euphrates? Or will it be the gods of the Amorites in whose land you now live? But as for me and my family, we will serve the LORD.

Materials Needed:
(4) Small envelopes numbered #1, #2, #3, and #4.
(1) Plate
(1) $50 Bill

Concept:

   Three volunteers are given a free choice of four numbered envelopes. The remaining envelope is kept by the performer. When the envelopes are opened, it is revealed that the ultimate prize is in the hands of the performer.

How to do it:

   The key to this effect is the fact that the $50 is never actually in any of the envelopes. It is concealed underneath the plate, between your hand and the plate (See Figure 1 - the $50 bill is behind the plate in the palm of the hand). After the volunteers select their envelopes, slide the remaining envelope off the edge of the plate, bringing the money out with it (See Figure 2). Be sure to keep the money concealed behind the envelope. When the envelope is opened, it will appear the $50 is coming from within (Figure 3).

Figure 1

Figure 2 - This is the back view of bringing the $50 out from behind the plate and envelope

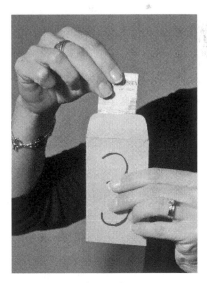

Figure 3

Presentation:

For this trick I am going to need three volunteers from the audience. And I am specifically looking for three people who are able to make a good decision (bring your three volunteers up to help you). Thank you for being willing to help me today.

Believe it or not, one of you today might win a $50 dollar bill! But, it is going to be up to you to make the right choice. On this plate there are four envelopes. In a moment each of you will have the opportunity to choose one of the envelopes. Then, we will find out if the envelope you chose has the $50 bill inside! (At this point, have each volunteer choose one envelope off the plate, but do not let them open it yet. It is especially fun to get the audience to yell out to the volunteers which envelope they think they should choose- like a game show).

Each one of you has made your choice, leaving me with one envelope left on the plate. Do you think you made the best choice today? You might be confident in your decision, but you might not be. I am going to give each of you the opportunity to change your mind and trade me for the envelope remaining on the plate (At this point, go back to the person who chose first and allow them to either keep their envelope or trade it for the one on the plate. After their decision, ask them to open the envelope they have selected and take out whatever is inside).

It looks like you did get something. Is it the $50 bill? No, I guess not. You did receive a gift certificate. That's a pretty good prize, but not the $50 bill. That means the $50 bill is still out there (have the first volunteer take their seat and allow the next volunteer to keep or trade their envelope. Then repeat the process of having them open it).

Let's see if they chose the $50 bill. Open your envelope! It is another gift certificate. Let's give them a round of applause

32

as well for helping (have the second volunteer take their seat. Take a moment to allow the suspense to build before immediately having the final volunteer open their envelope).

We have one more volunteer and two envelopes remaining. The $50 bill is still in play. Would you like to keep the envelope you chose previously, or would you like to trade it for the remaining envelope? Audience, what do you think she should do? (After the volunteer makes his or her decision, have them open their envelope. As they do this, slide the envelope you were left with off the back of the plate and bring the $50 bill out behind it. Then set the plate aside. The audience will be focusing on your volunteer opening their envelope. This will provide you with extra cover.) It looks like they did not win the $50 today either, but you can still clap your hands for this volunteer!

Each of our volunteers chose an envelope today. They then had the opportunity to change their minds, eventually leaving me with this envelope. Let's open it up and see what is inside (open up the envelope, and slide the $50 out from behind it. It will appear that the $50 bill is coming from inside the envelope). There is the $50 bill!

That was just a trick, and the reality is that none of these volunteers knew what the end result of their choice was going to be. There is a decision that each of us can make and know what the future result will be. The decision is choosing to live for Jesus.

If we make the choice to live for Jesus and make Him number one in our life, we can know for sure that one day we will spend eternity with Him in Heaven. And, even here on earth, we can experience the joy of a personal relationship with Him each and every day!

Tip:

We like the idea of preparing each envelope with some type of prize inside so that each volunteer does end up with something. It could be a $1 bill, a gift certificate for an ice cream cone, etc. This also strengthens the illusion as the audience believes each envelope did contain something, but only one had the $50 bill.

Chapter Six
Nothing Can Separate

Nothing can separate us from the love of Christ.

Verse: Romans 8:38-39 (New Living Translation)
And I am convinced that nothing can ever separate us from God's love. Neither death nor life, neither angels nor demons, neither our fears for today nor our worries about tomorrow—not even the powers of hell can separate us from God's love. No power in the sky above or in the earth below—indeed, nothing in all creation will ever be able to separate us from the love of God that is revealed in Christ Jesus our Lord.

Materials Needed:
Rubber Cement
Newspaper
Baby Powder
Scissors

Concept:
A strip of newspaper is folded in half. The fold is then cut out of the paper (figure #1), but when the newspaper is reopened it is still in one long piece (figure #2). The newspaper can repeatedly be folded and cut, but each time it is shown to remain intact.

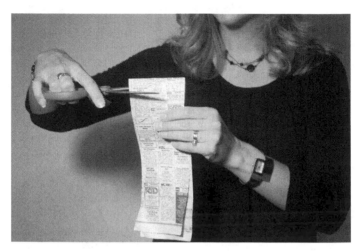

Figure #1

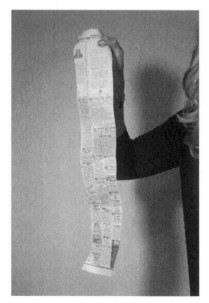

Figure #2

How to do it:

Before beginning the trick, prepare the strip of newspaper by covering the center section in rubber cement (on one side only - Figure #3). Be sure to cover the strip completely to the edges. Then, lightly spread some baby powder over the rubber cement (Figure #4). This should just be a small amount to keep the paper from sticking together when it is folded in half. Now, when you fold the newspaper in half, as long as you cut within the section you previously covered in rubber cement the newspaper will automatically reattach.

Figure #3   Figure #4

Presentation:

A simple piece of newspaper. At least, that is what it looks like. I have discovered something interesting about this newspaper. Most of the time when you cut a piece of paper it falls in half, but not this one. Some of you may doubt this is true, so let me show you. If I take this piece of newspaper and a pair of scissors, fold the paper in half, and then cut it (fold and cut the newspaper) it should come a part. But, as you can see, when I open the newspaper (open it back up) it is still in one long strip. Let's try that again. I fold the paper, cut it, and it should come apart. Once again, it is still connected!

This reminds me of a great thing we learn about in the book of Romans. In chapter eight we learn that nothing can ever separate us from God's love. Even when we face trouble, are hungry or cold (fold and cut the newspaper, then show it to be restored), we cannot be separated from His love. If we are persecuted, face danger or even death (again, fold and cut the paper. Open it to show it is still one long piece) - nothing can ever separate us from the love of Jesus Christ.

You can be sure that no matter what obstacles or circumstances you face in your life. Jesus will always be there for you and nothing can ever separate us from His love!

Helpful Hints:
1.   After covering the inside section of the newspaper with rubber cement and baby powder you will notice that some residue will remain. Be sure to keep this part of the paper facing toward you during your performance and keep the unblemished side facing your audience.
2.   Make sure to pay attention to how much of the paper you covered in rubber cement and be careful not to cut beyond this section. The amount of rubber cement you use will determine how long ahead of time you can prepare this (after too long the rubber cement will no longer be strong enough to reconnect). Be sure you experiment by preparing the sheet of paper and setting it aside for at least as long as you will need to have it prepared in advance of your performance.

3.   It is best to use the classified section of the newspaper or a section with a lot of text. This way when the paper rejoins itself it will still look normal.

Chapter Seven
The Unseen

Our focus and greatest concern should be on what matters for eternity.

There are times when we want to reinforce that everything we do is just an illusion. The first part of this trick is a great way for people to see how there is always more happening in the illusion than what they can see. For a moment, they are even taught how then can do their own illusion. But, in the end, there is still an extra special finish.

Verse: II Corinthians 4:18 (NIV)
For we fix our eyes not on what is seen, but on what is unseen. For what is seen is temporary, but what is unseen is eternal.

Materials Needed:
(1) Pencil
(1) Small fingernail file

Concept:
A pencil is displayed to the audience in a closed fist. As the presenter's hand slowly opens the pencil appears to be floating (figure #1). The audience is apparently shown the secret behind the effect, only to be tricked once again (figure #4).

Figure #1

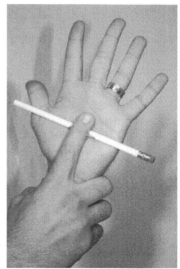

Figure #2

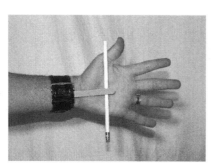

Figure #3

Figure #4

How to do it:

The first time the pencil appears to be levitating; it is actually being held in place by the first finger of your opposite hand (figure #2). The second time, secure a file between the band of your watch and your wrist to hold the pencil in place (figure #3). A very fun and astonishing trick!

Presentation:

Take a moment and focus your eyes right here at the pencil I have in my hand. If you watch closely, something interesting will happen (begin to slowly open your hand, one finger at a time, until the pencil appears to be floating behind your fingers). If you continue to focus carefully, it may just appear to you that the pencil is actually floating! Is this reality? Or is it just an illusion? (Turn your hand around to reveal the secret- the finger on your other hand holding the pencil in place).

There are times when each of us becomes so convinced that something is real or true. At one point or another, each of us have probably been tricked and deceived into thinking the things of this world are more important than they are. We begin to get so focused on fitting in, being popular, and on worldly possessions that we forget where our real focus needs to be.

Do not let anyone confuse you. Our concern should be on what will make an eternal difference- anything else is just an illusion (show the pencil floating again- this time take your back hand away and let the file be the lone support).

Helpful Hints:

When you begin this trick the file should already be in place (you can also use another pencil or other object in place of the file). This way you are immediately set up for the second part of the trick. Because the file is already in place, be extra careful to keep it covered up when you turn your hand around to show "the secret" the first time.

If you perform or teach in the same place or for the same audience several times, you may wish to not even show them how the first part of the trick is done. After several different times showing them the "floating pencil", you can then show them the secret behind it (your other finger holding it). Now, when you take that hand away, it will really create an amazing illusion!

Chapter Eight
WHATEVER!

Focus your mind on what is truly important.

Verse: Philippians 4:8 (NIV)
　　　Finally, brothers, whatever is true, whatever is noble, whatever is right, whatever is pure, whatever is lovely, whatever is admirable- if anything is excellent or praiseworthy- think about such things.

Materials Needed:
(1) Box of no more than eight crayons.

Concept:
　　　A volunteer chooses any one of eight colors and places it behind your back in your hand. With the crayon still behind your back, you are able to tell exactly which color has been selected.

How to do it:
1.　　　When the volunteer places the crayon in your hand behind your back, simply use your fingernail to scrape a small speck off the crayon (figure #1).

2.　　　Keep the crayon in one hand behind your back, and take the other hand (with the speck on your fingernail) and bring it forward. Touch your finger to your head as if you are concentrating hard (figure #2). As you bring your finger up toward your head, glance at your fingernail to see what color you have scraped off.

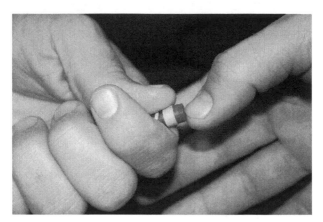

Figure #1

Figure #2

Presentation:

Today I would like to share with you my amazing ability to read somebody's mind. To do this, I am going to need a volunteer to help me (choose a volunteer, and have them place one crayon in your hand behind your back without you seeing). Now, I would like you to focus on the color of the crayon that you have selected, but please do not say it. I am going to see if I can read your mind and discover what color you have selected (play this up- pretend to really focus for a moment before you name the color.

Ask your volunteer if you were correct, then bring your other hand forward to reveal to the entire crowd the crayon they had placed in your hand). The reality is that I cannot truly read anyone's mind. That was just a trick. Even though I do not know your thoughts, there is someone who does. That person is Jesus Christ.

Jesus does know our every thought and He wants us to keep our thoughts pure and right. In fact, Philippians 4:8 tells us to focus our minds on things that are true, noble, right, pure, lovely, admirable, excellent, and praiseworthy. Make sure that today you keep your mind focused on things that please Him!

Helpful Hints:

If there are too many colors, or the colors are too similar, this can be very difficult. For this reason it is better to only use a few colors and make sure they are all different.

Practice this trick in the exact same environment you wish to perform it in. If you are in a place where stage or sunlight is shining in your eye, it will be very difficult to see the color on your finger nail. Last, try this out a few different times experimenting with using different finger nails and even your thumb nail. This way you can decide what feels most natural and works best for you!

Chapter Nine
Accomplish The Impossible

With God, we can accomplish what we might have thought was impossible.

Verse: Luke 1:37 (New King James Version)
For with God nothing will be impossible.

Materials Needed:
Scissors
(1) Plain sheet of paper

Concept:
A normal piece of paper is displayed. Then, a hole is cut in the paper large enough for a person to walk through.

How to do it:
1.   Make a cut down the center of the paper. Do NOT cut all the way to the edges. To do this, you will have to first poke a small hole just inside the edge of the paper, then cut toward the opposite end, stopping before you cut all the way through (see figure #1 and #2 on the following page).

2.   Fold the paper in half along the cut.

| Figure #1 | Figure #2 |

3. Holding the folded paper in your hand, began alternating cuts from the right side of the paper, then below cutting it from the left side. Continue alternating your cuts from each side beginning at the top and moving down towards the bottom (Figure #3). When you are cutting, please remember to NOT completely cut all the way through the paper. You should cut from one side, but stop just before completing the cut on the opposite side. When you have done this all the way from the top to the bottom you should be able to open your paper up and have a nice big hole to walk through (Figure #4).

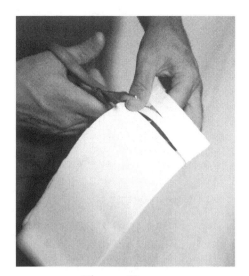

Figure #3

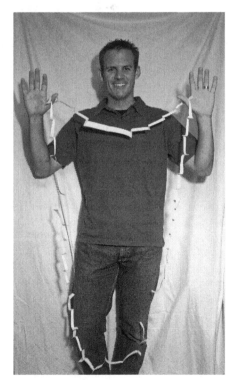

Figure #4

Presentation:

How many of you believe it is possible for me to cut a hole in this small piece of paper that would be large enough for me to walk through? It seems impossible, doesn't it? In fact, in our lives we will often face challenges and difficulties that make us feel it is impossible for us to go on or make it through. (Begin to cut the paper, according to the directions and Figures #1 and #2, as you continue to discuss some of the challenges we often face.)

The reality is that we all face different circumstances and challenges in our lives. Some of you might be facing a problem at school. Maybe you are doing your best to live the way God would want you to live and to be an example for others, but you feel like it is hard. People may discourage you and try to bring you down. There are times in our lives when people say hurtful things to us, even people that are close to us. It could be your friends, or even your parents who have said or done things that hurt you. You might in a situation where you are always trying your best, but you wonder if it is good enough. That might be the situation with your school work or the sports you like.

Sometimes we face even bigger challenges. Your parents might be going through a tough time, or they could be separated or divorced. In your family, somebody may have a sickness they are trying to overcome. The good news is this (open up the paper now to reveal the large hole you have made, Figure #4). No matter what obstacles or challenges we face in life, we can always know that God is there for us to go to and pray to about our struggles. Whatever your situation or challenge is, remember this: (begin walking through the piece of paper) in Luke 1:37 it says that with God nothing is impossible!

Helpful Hints:

The closer together you make your cuts, the larger the circle will be for you to walk through. You can make the cuts so close together that several people can walk through the paper. But, the closer the cuts are together the weaker the paper becomes and more likely it is to tear if you snag it somehow when walking through. For this reason, card stock or construction paper is good. Heavier paper is stronger.

Make sure to practice giving your message when you make the cuts. The length of your message could vary greatly depending on how close your cuts are, so it is important to be prepared with what you are planning to say.

Chapter Ten
Captured By His Love

No matter what we do or have done, God will never stop loving us.

Verse: Hebrews 13:5-6 (NIV)

Keep your lives free from the love of money and be content with what you have, because God has said, "Never will I leave you; never will I forsake you." So we say with confidence, the Lord is my helper; I will not be afraid. What can man do to me?"

Materials Needed:

(1) Solid Metal Ring

(1) 36" piece of chain or rope

Concept:

    The ends of a chain are held in one hand, with the middle of the chain hanging down. A solid ring is placed over the center of the chain. When the ring is dropped it will fall off the chain, but whenever the performer desires he or she can make the ring attach itself to the chain.

How to do it:

    At the moment the ring is dropped from the performer's hands, the front edge of the ring is pushed downward and back through the loop of chain. This causes the ring to turn over and become intertwined in the chain (Figures 1-6 demonstrate this progression. During the actual performance your hand does NOT stay in contact with the ring the entire time. Rather, you simply flip the bottom of the ring forward and through the chain. These pictures are here to help you visualize the progression).

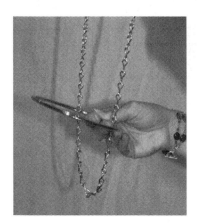

Figure 1

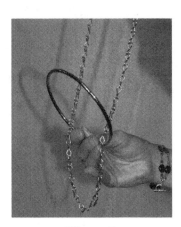

Figure 2

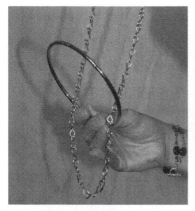

Figure 3

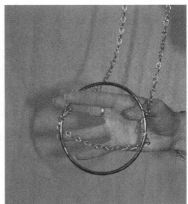

Figure 4

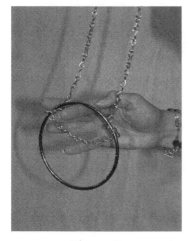

Figure 5

Figure 6

Presentation:

Have you ever wondered what we as people can do to make God stop loving us? When I think about my life, I know that even though I try to do my best, there are times when I still mess up. Is it possible for us to mess up so badly that God will stop loving us and abandon us? Today, we are going to see if we can answer that question.

To help us do this we are going to try an experiment using this ring and chain (hand the ring and the chain out to the audience and let them examine them). This ring is going to represent a person just like me and you. We often go around and around trying our best to get things right. This chain is going to represent God's love. We may sometimes feel like we are here in God's love (place the ring around the chain), when we are doing well. But, then we might mess up. You might even say that we fall. When we fall it is easy to think that we reach a place where God no longer loves us (allow the ring to fall off the loop of chain to the floor or table).

Some people might tell you that God no longer loves this person because he has messed up, and now he must try again to be a good enough and nice enough person to get back to a place that God would love him (place the ring back around the loop of chain). But, even if this person could be good for a while, there will certainly come another time where he will fall again (drop the ring off of the loop onto the floor or table once more). The reality is that God does love each and every one of us.

Amazingly, He loves us even when we mess up. We should definitely do our best to live in a way that pleases God, but the good news for today is that even when we mess up God will not stop loving us.

Let's try this experiment one more time and see if we can achieve a different result (place the ring around the chain once more). When we live our life for Jesus we can know that he will never stop loving us. In fact, even when we fall (drop the ring, this time pushing the front of the ring downward and through the loop so it will latch on) we will be captured by His love! God has said "Never will I leave you; never will I forsake you." No matter what you have done, what mistakes you have made, and what sins you have committed. God still loves you and can do great things in your life!

Helpful Hints:

Do your best to drop the ring with a similar motion both when you want the ring to fall off the chain and when you want it to attach to the chain.

Chapter Eleven
Set Free From Sin

If we confess our sin, God will forgive us.

Verse: I John 1:9 (NIV)

If we confess our sins, He is faithful and just and will forgive us our sins and purify us from all unrighteousness.

Materials Needed:

(1) Solid Metal Ring
(1) 36" piece of chain or rope
(1) Handkerchief

Concept:

A ring is "tied" on a rope illustrating how each of us is held captive by sin. Two volunteers hold the ends of the rope. The ring is covered momentarily by a handkerchief, and then shown to have been removed from the rope.

How to do it:

Before beginning the trick, place the ring on the rope by holding the ends in one hand with the center of the rope hanging down. Pull the middle of the rope through the ring, then push the ends of the rope between the ring and the loop of rope (see Figure 1). This will make it look like the ring is tied on the rope (Figures 2 and 3). Under the cover of the handkerchief, simply pull the center loop of the rope down and around the ring to release it. Make sure your volunteers give you plenty of slack in the rope (Figure 4). Once the ring is released, pull away the handkerchief that was covering it with a flourish and you are finished (Figure 5)!

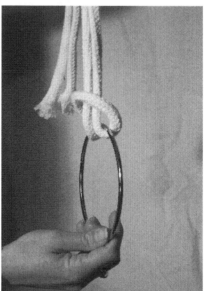

Figure 1

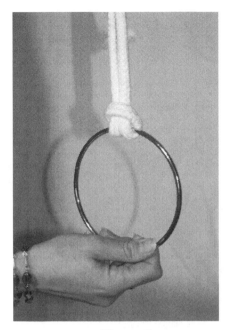

Figure 2

Figure 3

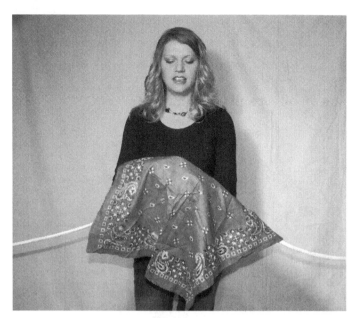

Figure 4

Figure 5

Presentation:

Have you ever done something you knew you were not supposed to do? All of us have. Maybe you took something that did not belong to you. You might have said something you should never have said. It is even possible that you simply thought something in your mind or had harmful intentions that you never should have. These are some of the things that the Bible calls sin.

The reality is that each and every one of us has sinned. Because we have sinned we have been separated from God, and there is even a price that we owe. The bible tells us that the wages of sin, or the price that we owe, is death (Romans 6:23). Just like this chain is tightly holding onto this ring, the sin in our lives holds us captive too.

I am going to have a volunteer hold onto each end of the chain to make sure the ring can not be removed from either side (have a volunteer come up and take each end). Each of us may feel the chains of sin in our life, but we can be set free. The wages of sin is death, but the gift of God is eternal life! Jesus paid the price for us when he died on the cross for our sins and then rose from the grave.

I John I:9 says that if we confess our sins, He is faithful and just to forgive us of our sin and cleanse us from all unrighteousness. (Cover the ring with the cloth) No matter what type of sin we have committed if we ask Jesus to forgive us, He can set us free (remove the ring from the chain and the cross and hold it high for everyone to see)!

Helpful Hints:

When your volunteers hold the ends of the chain, make sure you keep some slack in the chain. If the chain is pulled too tightly it will be difficult to remove the ring.

Chapter Twelve
The One And Only

Jesus is the only way to get to Heaven. When you accept Jesus into your life, you can know for sure you will spend eternity with Him!

Verse   John 14:6 (New Living Translation)

Jesus told him, "I am the way, the truth, and the life. No one can come to the Father except through me."

Materials Needed:

(5) Checkers

(1) Marker

(6) Stick-on labels (cut small enough to fit on the checkers)

(1) Envelope

(1) Piece of paper

Concept:

Five checkers are displayed, as well as a prediction. Four of the checkers are eliminated, and the remaining checker matches the prediction.

How to do it:

All five of the checkers are labeled on one side, but one is actually labeled on both sides. The one labeled on both sides will be the predicted checker (Figure #4). No matter how many times it is dropped, it can never land face down!

Figure #1

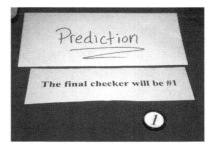

Figure #2

Figure #3

Figure #4

Presentation:

Here are five checkers that are numbered #1, #2, #3, #4, and #5. Believe it or not, I have made a prediction and sealed it inside this envelope about one of these checkers (display the sealed envelope with your prediction and keep it in full view - Figure #1). What I would like you to do is take these checkers in your hand, shake them up, and then drop them out onto the table (Figure #2). The ones that are face down will be eliminated; the ones that land with the number face up will still be in play (Figure #3). We will continue to do this until only one checker remains (have your volunteer continue this process as many times as necessary until only one checker remains).

All of the checkers have now been eliminated except one, and that is the number "1". For the first time, open up the envelope and show us the prediction that is inside. The prediction says "the final checker will be #1" (Figure #4).

Of course, that was just a trick. I really cannot predict the future. But, there is one thing I do know for sure. I know that one day I will spend eternity with Jesus in Heaven. This is something we can all know for sure. In John 14:6 Jesus says "I am the way the truth and the life, no one comes to the father but by me." The final checker was #1. This can also be a reminder that there is only one way to get to Heaven, and that is Jesus.

If we choose to accept Jesus and make him #1 in our lives, we can know for sure that we will be in Heaven with Him. We definitely cannot know everything about the future, but knowing how to get to Heaven is something great to know!

Helpful Hints:

You can choose to make any checker be the final prediction by labeling it on both sides, but we like using #1 to help reinforce the message.

After the volunteer drops the checkers, make sure you are the one that picks the remaining checkers up each time and places them in the volunteer's hands. Otherwise, there is a greater chance the volunteer will notice one double-sided checker.

Pay attention to the surface of the table you use to perform the trick. If the checkers roll around on it quite a bit before falling flat, or if they can easily fall off the table, it increases the chance of someone seeing the double-sided checker.

Chapter Thirteen
The Meaning Of Life

It is easy to get distracted by the things of this world, but in the end only one thing matters- having a personal relationship with Jesus Christ.

Verse: Matthew 16:26 (New Living Translation)
And what do you benefit if you gain the whole world but lose your own soul? Is anything worth more than your soul?

Materials Needed:
(6) Identical Envelopes, number four of them 1-4 (Figure #1)
(4) Identical pictures representing Jesus (Figure #2)
(4) Different pictures representing worldly possessions (Fig. #3)
Scissors

Figure #1

Figure #2   Figure #3

Figure #4   Figure #5

Concept:

    A volunteer is given their free choice of four envelopes. The envelope they choose will represent what life is all about and how we find true purpose and meaning. The three envelopes they do not choose are opened to reveal worldly possessions. The envelope they did choose is opened to show a picture representing Jesus Christ.

How to do it:

Each envelope is gimmicked and has two pockets (Figure #4). The picture of Jesus is in one pocket and another picture is in the separate pocket. So, no matter what envelope is chosen it will produce a picture of Jesus.

Create these pockets with the two extra envelopes. Simply cut the back of the envelope off and trim it just a bit so it fits inside another envelope.

Presentation:

It is time to answer the question- what is life all about? Have you ever thought about that? There are so many things in life that demand our attention, but what is most important? What is life really all about? Today we are going to do our best to answer that question.

Inside each of these envelopes is something that will help us better understand what life is all about. The envelopes are numbered 1, 2, 3, and 4 (Figure #1). I need a volunteer to select one of these envelopes (choose your volunteer). It is up to you to make a very important decision. Whichever envelope you select is the one that will have the answer to the question- what is life all about? Which one would you like to use? (We will say they select #4).

Before we look at what is inside the envelope our volunteer selected, let's see what he is missing out on. Inside envelope #1 is- money! And that is what life is all about, right? Getting as much money as you can! No, that's not it. Inside envelope #2 is… games and toys. Is that what life is all about- having all the latest and greatest toys? No, that is not it either. Let's check out #3. Here we have- a star! That's right- life is all about being a star, being popular, and getting people to like you! No, that really is not it either.

71

Sometimes having money, having the coolest toys, and being popular seem to be pretty important. But the truth is they are not what life is all about. In fact, in Matthew 16:26 the Bible asks us what good would it be if we gained the whole world but lost our soul? We can have all of these things, but there is something much more important. Without it, all those other things would be worthless.

Our volunteer selected #4. When I take this picture out, if this represents what life is really all about- then you can clap your hands. (Remove the picture of Jesus - Figure #5). I am so glad our volunteer made the right choice today. Jesus really is what life is all about and how we find purpose and meaning in our lives.

Helpful Hints:

Make sure you place all the Jesus pictures on the same side of the envelope (near the flap or away from the flap) so it is easy to remember exactly where it is (Figure #5 and #6). When the last envelope is opened, you can even hold the pocket closed and allow your volunteer to reach in and pull the picture out.

Chapter Fourteen
God Will Make A Way

When we are tempted to do wrong, we can trust that God will give us a way out.

Verse: I Corinthians 10:13 (New Living Translation)
The temptations in your life are no different from what others experience. And God is faithful. He will not allow the temptation to be more than you can stand. When you are tempted, he will show you a way out so that you can endure.

Materials Needed:
(1) Long piece of rope (approximately 7 feet)

Concept:
A rope is tied around the performer's neck (Figure #1). When the rope is pulled tight it passes right through the neck!

Figure #1

How to do it:

    The rope, of course, does not pass through your neck. After being placed over your head, a slip knot is formed (Figure #2 and #3). To do this, begin by placing the rope over your head and behind your neck so the ends are dangling down in front of you. Now, with your right hand, reach across your body and pinch the piece of the rope that is hanging down on the left side. Pull this part of the rope back across your body and in front of the rope on your right side.

    With your left hand, take the end of the rope hanging down on the right side. Bring it over the section you are holding with your right hand (creating a slip knot) and continue all the way over your head, bringing it to the left side. As you do this, the section of rope that was previous on your left will move slightly to the right in front of your neck. This creates the illusion of the rope being tied around your neck.

    When you pull on the ends of the rope the slip knot is released and the rope falls forward (Figure #4). The pictures explain this further. Be sure to practice this very slowly the first several times to make sure you are doing it correctly!

Figure #2

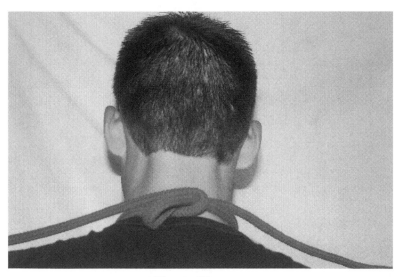

Figure #3

Presentation:

Every single one of us at one point or another find ourselves in a situation that we would rather not be in. (Begin placing the rope over your head - Figure #1. As you talk about the temptation and difficult situations we face, tie the rope into a slip knot - Figure #2. It will appear that the rope is being tied more securely around your neck - Figure #3). We take a step in a wrong direction down a path we should not be going on. After a while, we find that we are in a circumstance that has us held captive. Maybe we even find ourselves facing temptations that we think are impossible for us to resist. We might find ourselves in a place where we desperately need a way out!

In I Corinthians 10:13 God tells us that the temptations we face will not be more than what we can stand. And, when you are tempted, he will show you a way out so that you can endure. We will never be put into a position in which the temptations we face are too difficult for us.

The next time you are tempted, make sure you turn to God and prayer and know that He will show you (grab both ends of the rope and pull, creating the illusion that the rope passes through your neck) a way out (Figure #4)!

Figure #4

Helpful Hints:

You definitely want to practice this several times very slowly to be sure that you know what you are doing! When you do pull the rope back over your head and create the slip knot, you can keep your finger temporarily inside the loop of the slip knot so the rope will not fall forward too quickly. As long as your finger is still inside the loop, the rope will not release. Which means you can very effectively create the illusion of the rope being held tightly to your neck. This trick will definitely get their attention! But, once again- be careful!

Chapter Fifteen
The Plans

We may not know the future, but we can know that God has great plans for each and every one of us!

Verse: Jeremiah 29:11 (NIV)

For I know the plans I have for you," declares the Lord, "plans to prosper you and not to harm you, plans to give you hope and a future.

Materials Needed:
(3) 8" x 11" pieces of white card stock
(1) 5" x 7" pieces white card stock
(1) Envelope
(1) Marker
(1) Piece of paper
Clear Tape

Concept:

An audience member is shown three sheets of paper (numbered 1, 2, and 3) and asked to freely name one of the numbers. The presenter is able to immediately reveal that he/she had correctly predicted which number would be selected.

How to do it:

The secret to this trick is to have a separate prediction in three different places. To set this up, tape the small 5" x 7" pieces of paper to the middle of the larger sheets. Only tape the pieces on the top. This enables you to lift the 5" x 7" piece up (like a flap) and show what is underneath.

For this illustration, on the back of card number one was the prediction "you will choose 1" (Figure #1). Under the front flap of card two was the prediction "you will choose 2" (Figure #2). Finally, if the audience member had chosen number three, the attention would be directed to a sealed envelope off to the side. After opening the envelope, a prediction would be revealed "you will choose 3" (Figure #3). The key to this last part is not to mention the envelope until you need to. That way, if the participant selects one or two, you never have to mention the envelope, and nobody will even realize it had a purpose in the trick. But, if they choose three and are then asked to open the sealed prediction, the trick is even more amazing!

Figure #1

Figure #2

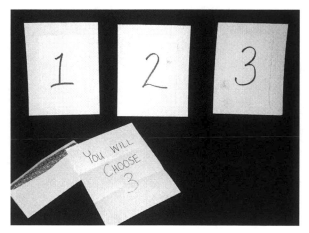

Figure #3

Presentation:

Right now I am going to demonstrate for you something amazing- my ability to predict the future! On display before you are three numbered cards. In a moment one of you will have the opportunity to name any one of the three cards, after which I will reveal my prediction to be correct (At this time have some fun selecting your volunteer. You may wish to toss a foam ball or something else into the audience to ensure the fact that the volunteer is randomly selected and in no way could have been prearranged. After the volunteer is chosen, ask them to name out loud one of the three numbers. For the example, we will say they select number 1).

Our volunteer had a free choice of three numbers and selected number 1. Believe it or not, on the back of this card I did predict- "you will choose 1". Now, some of you may think the prediction was on the back of all three cards (begin to turn the other cards around as well, revealing them to be blank), but it was only there behind number 1.

Can I really predict the future? No, that is just an illusion. But even though we may not know our future, we can know that God has some great things in store for each of us. In fact, in Jeremiah 29:11 God says "I know the plans I have for you- plans to prosper you and not to harm you." We can know that if we choose to follow God's plan for our life, we will truly experience some amazing things!

Helpful Hints:

Once again, remember to have the envelope somewhere in sight, but do not draw any further attention to it unless your volunteer chooses "3". After your volunteer names their number aloud, be sure to confirm their selection before you reveal it.

Another good thing to remember is that if your volunteer selects "1" or "2", show the predicted number first, then the other of the two ("1" or "2"), and show "3" last. This is because there is absolutely no writing either on the back or under the flap of number "3". If the selection was "2", for example, I would first lift the flap to show the prediction "you will select 2". The audience immediately wonders about the other numbers. So, I would show underneath the flap for #1, and then pick up #3, and show it more thoroughly before setting it back down.

Chapter Sixteen
Messed Up?

We all make mistakes and sometimes get a little turned around in life. When life gets confusing we can turn to God's word as a light to guide us.

Verse: Psalm 119:105
(New Living Translation)
Your word is a lamp to guide my feet and a light for my path.

Materials Needed:
(7) One Dollar Bills
Rubber Cement

Concept:
(5) one dollar bills are shown face up. Then, the bills are mixed up so some are face up and some are face down. The packed is squared up, and the performer is immediately able to spread the bills out and show that they are all once again face up.

How to do it:
Although it looks like you have (5) one dollar bills, there are actually seven. The secret is in the preparation. Before beginning, use the rubber cement to stick two of the bills back to back. Make sure George Washington's head is facing up on both sides. Repeat this process with two more bills (Figure #1). This should give you three regular one dollar bills and two of the gimmicked bills (made up of two bills each).

Figure #1

Begin by stacking these "five" bills together face up, with the gimmicked bills in the 2nd and 4th position (Figure #2 and Figure #3 - bottom view). As you show your audience the five bills begin by sliding the top bill off with your right hand as in Figure #2. You now will have four dollar bills remaining in your left hand and one in your right. Turn both hands over to show the backs (you are really showing the back of the bottom bill in your left hand - Figure #4).

Figure #2   Figure #3 (view from the bottom)

Figure #4   Figure #5

Lay the dollar in your right hand down, and then drop the 2nd dollar bill on top of it. Now, take the 3rd bill off in your right hand, turn over both hands, and drop the 3rd bill on top of the current pack. Place the 4th bill on top, and then finally show the 5th dollar bill on both sides.

After showing the bills, pick the pile back up and spread it out. Now, turn the non-gimmicked dollar bills (1st, 3rd, and 5th position) face down (Figure #5). At this point all that is left to do is square the packet back up, turn the entire thing over an odd number of times (Figures #6 and #7), and show that they are back in order (Figure #2).

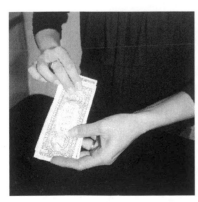

Figure #6   Figure #7

Presentation:

I don't know about you, but I really like it when things are in the correct order and easy to understand. Wouldn't it be great if everything was always just the way it should be and all of our decisions were clear and easy? It would certainly be nice if everything was always in perfect order just the way we like it.

Take these dollar bills, for instance. I have five dollar bills (count and display the bills "on both sides" as in the instructions - Figure #2) and right now they are all in perfect order. They are all heads up and facing the same direction. I like to keep my money like this so it is easy for me to know how much money I have, and so I can easily find the amount I need. But, sometimes my money gets a little messed up (turn over the bills in the 1st, 3rd, and 5th position - Figure #5).

I suppose this is somewhat like life can be. We want things to go perfectly according to our plan. We want everything to happen in just the right way, and in the perfect order. But, sometimes life takes a twist and a turn and we realize the plan and the steps we had planned out are now more confusing and out of order. When we are not sure what to do next, it is always best to seek the Lord! In fact, God has given us the Bible to help guide us. Psalm 119:105 says His word is a lamp to guide our feet and a light for our path.

If we are willing to seek God through praying and reading the Bible daily, he will guide us. Even when life takes those crazy twists and turns (turn the five bills over an odd number of times- Figures #6 and #7), if we follow God's path we can know everything will always be in perfect order (display the bills all back in order - Figure #2)!

Helpful Hints:

When you turn the normal bills face down, practice doing this lengthwise rather than sideways. This way the bills will not only be face up at the end, but George Washington will be facing the same direction too. Also- be careful not to let anyone examine these dollar bills (and don't accidentally spend them)!

Chapter Seventeen
A Fruitful Life

Our life can be filled with abundant blessings when we choose to live for Jesus Christ.

Galatians 5:22-23 (NIV)
But the fruit of the Spirit is love, joy, peace, patience, kindness, goodness, faithfulness, gentleness, and self-control. Against such things there is no law.

Materials Needed:
(2) Paper lunch sacks
(1) Bottle of glue
(1) Marker
(18) Pieces of paper (approximately 3" x 6" each)
Scissors

Concept:
An empty paper bag is shown as an illustration of an empty life. That "life" is then filled with pieces of paper representing the difficulties and problems of this world. Each piece of paper has a different negative word written on it. The words on the paper are then transformed from negative things, into the fruits of the spirit as a representation of how our lives can be filled with the good things of Christ.

How to do it:
To do this trick, you need to prepare one of the paper bags with two secret compartments. To do this, cut one of the paper bags in half (see Figure #1 and #2) and place glue on the narrow sides of the bag and the bottom (Figure #3 and #4). The two other sides that are not glued will serve as the secret

compartments. Slide the glued half of the paper bag inside the other full bag (Figure #5). Press firmly on the glued sides and bottom to create your hidden pocket (Figure #6 and #7). You may need to slightly trim the top of the inside bag so it does not stick up over the top of the outer bag. At the beginning of the trick, load the "fruit of the spirit" words in one of the empty pockets (Figure #7).

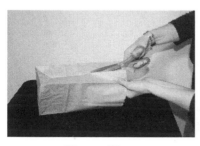
Figure #1

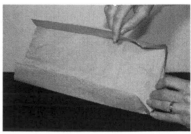
Figure #2

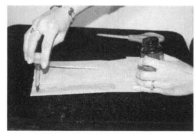
Figure #3

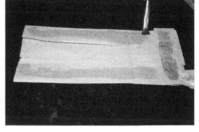
Figure #4

Figure #5

Figure #6

Figure #7

Figure #8

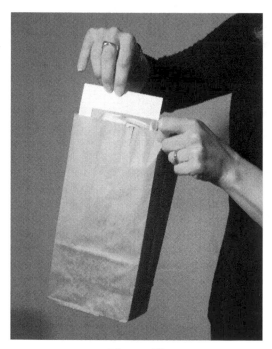

Figure #9

Presentation:

Before I knew Jesus, my life was empty- much like this paper bag (hold the paper bag up for all to see inside. Keep your hands over the secret compartments so that they are not revealed - Figure #8). In fact, there were many things that I struggled with. For example, I struggled with anger. I also struggled with envy, selfishness, emptiness, jealousy, and much more. My life was full of loneliness, sadness, bitterness, and bad thoughts (As each word is mentioned, display the paper with that word for your audience to see. Then place the words down into one of the secret compartments - Figure #9). But, when I handed all of those things over to him, Jesus did something amazing.

He took my life and transformed it. He brought me love. He began to bring me joy. He took my emptiness and gave me peace, patience, kindness, and gentleness. He has been teaching me more and more about faithfulness, gentleness, and self-control (pull the words with the fruit of the spirit on them out from the secret compartment they were loaded into before the trick began). My life truly is no longer empty. With Jesus, it is filled with abundance!

With Jesus I have everything! This does not mean that my life is now perfect and I never have any struggles. In this life, we may still have problems. But Jesus can give us His joy everyday. I hope and pray that you too have Jesus in your life!

Helpful Hints:

A paper bag seems completely innocent to an audience, which really aids in making this trick effective. When showing the inside of the bag to your audience, be sure to put one hand over each pocket and keep it pinched closed (Figure #8). There are a lot of different illustrations you can do using this bag. You can put a one dollar bill in and turn it into ten dollars. Write different sins on pieces of paper, place them inside, and then produce duplicate blank pieces demonstrating how God can wash us white as snow. Be creative with this, and you will discover many uses!

Chapter Eighteen
Priceless!

Each of us is extremely valuable to God! In fact, God loved us so much that He even sent His son Jesus to die for us.

Verse: Romans 5:8 (NIV)
But God demonstrates His own love for us in this way: While we were still sinners, Christ died for us.

Materials Needed:
(1) 6' piece of rope (preferably red)
(1) White cloth
(2) Duplicate "price tags"

Concept:
A price tag is shown as a representation of the fact that each of us is valuable to God (Figure #1). The price tag is then threaded onto a rope as an illustration that we are all held captive by sin. For a moment, the price tag is covered with a cloth (Figure #2). When the cloth is removed, the price tag has been "set free" and is unharmed.

Figure #1

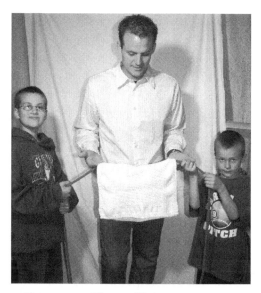

Figure #2

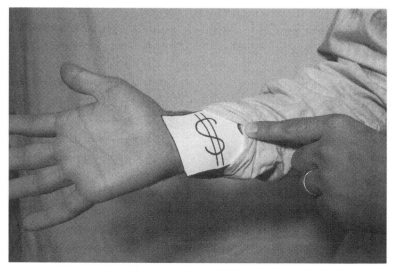

Figure #3

How to do it:

This time, it really is "up your sleeve". For this trick you need to wear long sleeves. In your preparation for the trick, be sure that the two price tags you have are exactly the same. Place one of the price tags up your sleeve (Figure #3). Then, when you reach the point in the trick where you cover the price tag with the cloth, you will tear the price tag that is on the rope to remove it (Figure #4). After removing the first tag, simply exchange it with the intact tag in your sleeve (Figure #5). After the cloth is removed, it will appear to your audience that the price tag has somehow penetrated the rope and is unharmed (Figure #1).

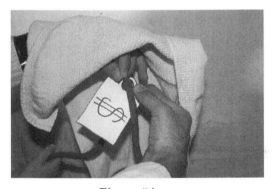

Figure #4

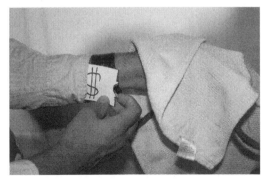

Figure #5

Presentation:

(Begin by bringing two volunteers up from the audience). I am so thankful that the two of you are willing to help me today because today we have something very special. First of all, I want to tell you both that you are extremely valuable. Now, when you go to a store, valuable things often have a price tag on them. Today we are going to be using this big price tag to represent your life (Figure #1).

Of course, it has to be a big price tag because there is no way we could truly put a price on how much your life is worth. God thinks our life is valuable, too. In fact, it is so valuable to Him that He would be willing to die for us.

You see, there is a problem. The problem is that each of us is held captive by sin. Today this red rope is going to represent sin. (Begin threading the price tag onto the rope, and have each volunteer hold one end of the rope). The Bible tells us that our sin is like scarlet- which is a red color. The truth is that there is nothing that we can do on our own to get rid of that sin.

Just like it seems it would be impossible to take this price tag off the rope without harming it. But, there is a way. Jesus came into the world to pay the price for our sin (Cover the price tag with the cloth - Figure #2). Though our sin was like scarlet, we can be washed as white as snow. If we are willing to accept the price Jesus paid for us when He died on the cross for our sin and then rose from the grave, we can be set free!

Chapter Nineteen
Wages And Gifts

We have all been separated from God because of our sin. Jesus alone was perfect, died for our sins, and rose from the grave. If we accept Him, we can be restored to a relationship with God.

Verse: Romans 3:23 (NIV)

All have sinned and fall short of the glory of God.

Romans 6:23 (New Living Translation)

For the wages of sin is death, but the free gift of God is eternal life through Jesus Christ our Lord.

Materials Needed:

(1) Piece of string or yarn (approximately 36")
(1) Red straw (secretly prepared with a cut down one side)
Scissors

Concept:

A piece of string is threaded through a straw and is clearly seen to be hanging out of both ends (Figure #2). The straw is then cut in half, apparently cutting the string as well. A moment later both pieces of the straw are seen separately, but the string is now restored.

Figure #1

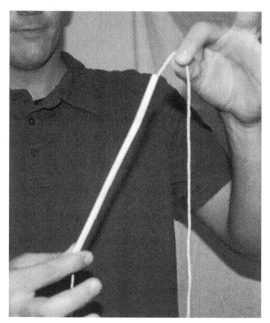

Figure #2

Figure #3

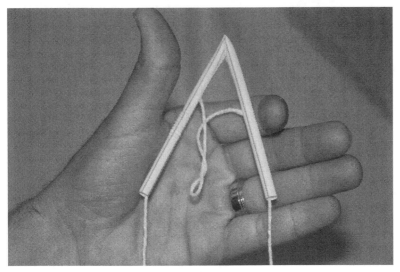

Figure #4

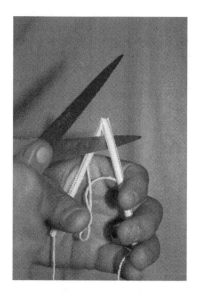

| Figure #5 | Figure #6 |

How to do it:

  The straw is prepared ahead of time with a cut down one side. This cut should be in the middle of the straw, about four inches long. This way, when the straw is bent in half, the string slides down through the cut and is covered by your hand (make sure the cut side is down before bending the straw). When the straw is cut it appears that the string has been separated as well (Figure #6). Now, simply hold the straw and string together tightly for a moment, and then open your hand to reveal the string is still intact (Figure #1). Amazing!

Presentation:

  It is amazing to know that each and every one of us was created by God. And, we were created to have a strong and solid relationship with him (show the string, and pull gently on it to show it is solid - Figure #1). But, there is a problem. At one point or another we have all messed up. We have all done things that were wrong. When we mess up like that, the Bible calls it sin. In fact, the Bible tells us our sin is like scarlet- which is kind of a red color (hold up the straw and begin to thread the string through it - Figure #2). That sin has now entered our life. And, because of that sin, we have been separated from God (bend the straw in half - Figure #3. As this happens the string is secretly dropped down so it is covered by your hands - Figure #4. Cut the straw in half - Figure #5).

The good news is that there is a way in which that relationship with God can be put back together. That way is not through anything we have done on our own, but only through Jesus Christ. Jesus came into this world as a person just like you and me, but Jesus was the only person who never sinned. He was perfect, but chose to pay the penalty for our sins on the cross. He died, but on the third day rose from the grave.

If we are now willing to accept what Jesus did for us, then we no longer have to be separated from God. In fact, we can once again experience a perfect relationship with God (See figure #6, and then restored string - Figure #1).

Helpful Hints:

Be sure to practice bending the straw and pulling the string down so you can do this with ease. You may have to adjust the size of your cut to make this easier for you, depending on the size of your hands. Also, the straw does not need to be red to do the trick (of course!), but a solid color is better, so the audience cannot see the string inside and notice it is not there when the straw is cut.

Chapter Twenty
Answer The Call

Jesus has called us- will we answer?

Mark 16:15 (NIV)
He said to them, "Go into all the world and preach the good news to all creation."

Materials Needed:
(2) Identical Notebooks
(1) Knife
Masking Tape
(1) Cell Phone

Concept:

Two nine digit numbers are written down on a piece of notebook paper by two separate volunteers. A third volunteer adds the numbers together, resulting in a ten digit number. When this number is called- it is your cell phone that rings!

How to do it:

Prepare the notebook ahead of time by using the knife to cut the back cover off. Then replace it with a cover identical as the front. The notebook should now look the same on both sides (Figure 1). Before beginning write down two nine digit numbers that add up to your cell phone number (with area code) under one of the covers (Figure 2). Have your volunteers write their numbers under the opposite cover. When you move to the third volunteer secretly turn the notebook over so that the volunteer adds the numbers you secretly wrote down earlier.

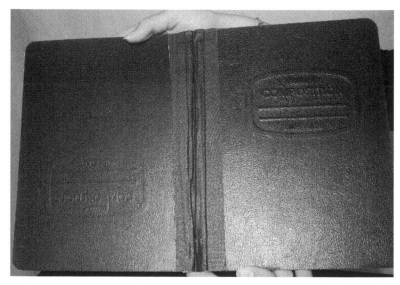

Figure 1

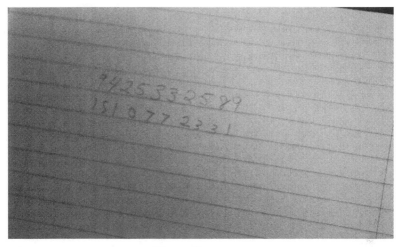

Figure 2

Presentation:

I thought it would be a lot of fun today for us to try a little experiment. What I am going to do is find a volunteer to write down on this notebook a number that has nine digits in it. For example: 422,376,185 is a number with nine digits. (Select your first volunteer. This is usually better to do by walking out to your audience instead of bringing somebody up on stage). Please do not tell anyone the number you are choosing- just write it down on this piece of notebook paper.

Let's go ahead and have another volunteer write a different nine digit number below this one (find another volunteer to do this). Now that we have two separate numbers, I need one more volunteer to use this calculator and add these two numbers together (move to the opposite side of the room for this volunteer and as you do turn the notebook over to the numbers you prepared ahead of time. This is important to minimize the possibility of one of the first two volunteers noticing that it is not the number they wrote down being added together).

The final number we come up with is a ten digit number. It is also interesting to note that if you include the area code our phone numbers are ten digit numbers too. I was thinking-wouldn't it be fun to go ahead and call this number that we came up with? It could be anyone! Maybe it is someone famous! Maybe even the President! Let's call and find out! (Have someone from the audience use their cell phone to call this final number. Either have your cell phone ring so you can answer, or you can have your voicemail pick up and say something like "Hi- this is (your name).

If today's experiment worked correctly, two random numbers were added together. Of the millions of numbers that could have resulted, it happened to be my cell phone! This experiment turned out to be amazing, but even more amazing is the message we have for you today.") It is incredible that you called me today. Even more amazing is the fact that today Jesus has called you! In fact, we are all called in one way or another to take the life changing message of Jesus to people everywhere.

You may be called to pray for those in need, to give or help in some way, you may even be called to go to another country. In Mark 16:15 Jesus said to go into all the world and preach the good news to all creation. God has an amazing plan for your life, are you willing to answer His call today?

Helpful Hints:

If you do not need ten digits to dial your cell phone, this will be easier by using two seven digit numbers that add up to your cell phone. It is best to use a calculator for this trick so your volunteer can quickly and accurately add the numbers written down. If using 10 digits, be sure to use a calculator that will display at least 10 digits.

Also, it may be best to simply record a message on your cell phone before the program rather than take the chance that somebody may call and disrupt the program at the wrong time!

Chapter Twenty-One
The Future

We cannot predict the future, but there is one thing we can know for sure- if we have accepted Jesus Christ as our Savior, we will one day spend eternity with Him in Heaven.

Verse: I Thessalonians 4:17
Then, together with them, we who are still alive and remain on the earth will be caught up in the clouds to meet the Lord in the air. There we will be with the Lord forever.

Materials Needed:
(2) Blank pieces of paper (Figure #1)
(1) Marker or Pen
(1) Envelope

Figure #1

Concept:

A prediction is made and sealed in an envelope. A volunteer chooses a number. After two quick steps, the final number is revealed to be exactly the same as the prediction in the sealed envelope.

How to do it:

This is an incredible trick because no matter what number your volunteer chooses, the prediction will always add up to 1,089. It is actually a simple math trick.

Have your volunteer choose any 3 digit number.

Take the number and reversed it and subtracted.

Then take the answer, reverse it again and added. The answer will always add up to 1,089. For example: 742-247= 495 + 594= 1,089.

Presentation:

How many of you think it is possible for me to predict the future? Some people might say that is impossible, but today I am going to try an experiment. Inside this envelope I have made a prediction. The envelope is now sealed, and I will not touch it again (you can even have a volunteer hold on to this envelope). Right now, I need a volunteer to select a number for us (Choose a volunteer and ask them to select a 3 digit number. Ask them to make sure that none of the numbers are the same. For example, it cannot be something like 444 or 717. Make sure they are all different. Write down the selected number on the paper).

Now, we are going to take the opposite of that number and subtract it, which gives us _____. Last, we will take the opposite of this number and add them together. This gives us an answer of 1089. For the very first time, please open the envelope! (The prediction in the sealed envelope is the number 1,089).

The truth is that I really cannot predict the future- that was just a trick. But, there is one thing each of us can know for sure about the future. We can know for sure that if we have accepted Jesus as our Lord and Savior, we will one day spend eternity with Him in Heaven!

Helpful Hints:

If the selected number is smaller than its reverse, simply subtract the smaller number. In the previous example, if a volunteer had selected 247, we would still begin by taking 742 – 247 to ensure we do not get a negative number.

It is also important that the numbers are not the same for this to work. Obviously, 333 – 333 = 0 and now the trick is over. The same is true for 818 or a similar number.

Last, if you get a number like 534. When you subtract 435 you end up with 99. In this situation, just make sure you keep 3 digits. In other words, write it as 099. 099 + 990= 1,089!

Try this a few times, and have some fun with it. You can even place your prediction in an envelope, and hang it from the ceiling or mail it to someone in advance (not to be opened). A great trick and a great message!

Chapter Twenty-Two
In A Moment

Our life on earth can end quickly- will you be ready for that moment?

Verse: I Corinthians 15:52 (New Living Translation)
It will happen in a moment, in the blink of an eye, when the last trumpet is blown. For when the trumpet sounds, those who have died will be raised to live forever. And we who are living will also be transformed.

Materials needed:
(1) Handkerchief
(2) Rings (one sewn to one side of the handkerchief, Figure #1)
(1) Paper bag
(1) Pencil

Concept:
A ring is displayed and wrapped inside a handkerchief. The ring is then vanished and later shown to have reappeared hanging on a pencil in the middle of a paper bag.

How to do it:
After showing the ring to the audience, place it underneath the handkerchief. When you place the ring behind the handkerchief, you actually are going to keep it concealed in your hand (Figure #2). While this ring is held in your hand, wrap the handkerchief around the ring that is sewn to the back of the handkerchief (Figure #3 and #4). Then place this ring in the hand of your volunteer (Figure #5). The volunteer is now holding on to the ring that is sewn to the handkerchief, but they think it is the original ring you had shown. As they continue to

hold the handkerchief, push the pencil through the center of the paper bag. As you push the pencil through the outside of the bag, put your hand with the original concealed ring inside the paper bag. Secretly thread the pencil through the original ring (Figure #6 and #7). The pencil is now sticking out of both sides of the paper bag, and the ring is inside (at this time unknown to your audience - Figure #8). Now, the tricky part is done.

Take both ends of the handkerchief and have your volunteer let go. When you pull the handkerchief away, it will seem the ring has disappeared! Have your volunteer now hold tightly to both ends of the pencil, and tear away the paper bag. Amazingly – the ring has reappeared (Figure #10 and #11)!

Figure #1

Figure #2

Figure #3

Figure #4

Figure #5

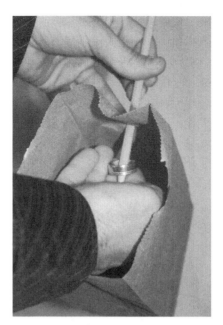

Figure #6

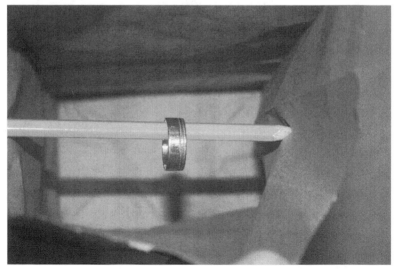

Figure #7

Figure #8

Figure #9

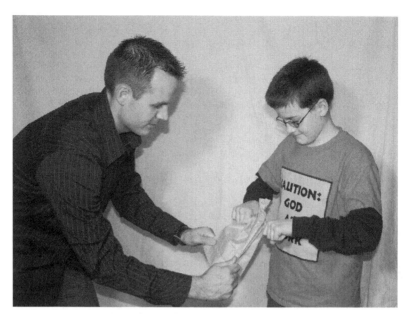

Figure #10

Figure #11

Presentation:

Today I want to show you something very special, something very important to me. I am going to need a volunteer to help me with this (get one volunteer from the audience). The special item we are going to be using today is my ring. Because this ring is so special to me, I want to take great care for it. So, I am going to wrap it up under this handkerchief (Figure #3). What I would like you to do is hold onto this nice and tight for me (Figure #5). We will come back to this in just a moment, but before we do, I have something else to show you. It is this paper bag.

What I am going to do is run this pencil right through the center of the paper bag (as you do this, place the ring onto the pencil - Figure #6 and #7). Are you still holding tight to what you have there? Good. You know, the ring you have there in your hands reminds me a lot of life. Life is very precious to us. Sometimes we think that we have such a good grip on it, and that we are in control. We may even think we know what is going to happen and when it is going to happen. But, are we really in control? No, life can change very quickly. In fact, what we thought we had complete control over can be immediately taken away from us (take the handkerchief back from your volunteer and quickly open it to reveal the ring has disappeared - figure #9).

Even though life can end in only a moment, we can know that is not the complete end of the story (at this point pick the paper bag up off of your table, and have your volunteer hold tightly onto the ends of the pencil that are hanging out the sides of the bag - Figure #10).

The Bible does tell us that in a moment, in the twinkling of an eye, the dead in Christ will rise and be raised to live forever with Jesus (as your volunteer holds the pencil, tear the bag away to reveal the ring is there - Figure #11). Even though our life on earth will end, we can know that when that happens we can rise and go to Heaven and spend eternity there!

Helpful Hints:

Make sure that the ring sewn inside the envelope is similar to the ring you are going to make vanish and reappear. If the audience sees has a ring with a diamond on it, the ring inside should also have a similar shape with some type of stone. Otherwise, the volunteer will notice the difference.

When you sew the duplicate ring to the handkerchief, keep it fairly close to a corner (Figure #1). This way, when you pull the handkerchief away, you can show it on both sides (keeping the ring concealed behind one hand).

Chapter Twenty-Three
Who Can God Use Most?

Each of us has been given different gifts by God. This does not mean that some people are better than others. God loves all of us the same and desires for us to come together and share our gifts.

Verse: I Corinthians 12:12 (New Living Translation)

The human body has many parts, but the many parts make up one whole body. So it is with the body of Christ.

Materials Needed:

(3) Equal length pieces of rope (approximately four feet each)

(3) Different colors of duct tape or electrical tape

Concept:

Three ropes are displayed. Each rope is tied into a separate circle. When all three circles are tossed into the air, they appear to transform into one large circle.

How to do it:

Begin by laying three pieces of rope in a large circle on the floor. Tape the ends that are next to each other with the same color (Figure #5). In other words, instead of having a rope with red tape on both ends, you will have one rope with a red and blue end, one with a blue and yellow end, and one with a yellow and red end. Hold the ropes in your hand with one red, yellow, and blue end up (Figure #1).

As you begin to tie the ends together, it will appear you are tying three separate circles. In reality, you are just tying the end of one rope to the end of the next. When tossed in the air, the ropes will come down as one large circle on their own. This is very visual and a great message!

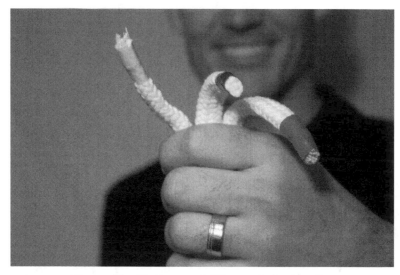

Figure #1 (Yellow end, Blue end, Red end)

Figure #2
In this figure you will tie the two red ends together. It appears to be the ends of the same rope, but is actually two different ropes.

Figure #3
Now, the ends of all three ropes are tied together. Continue to hold the ropes as if they are three separate loops.

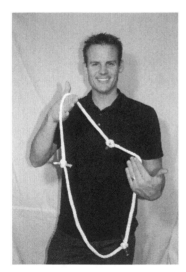

Figure #4

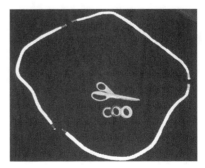

Figure #5 (Tape the ends of the rope that are next to each other with the same color)

Presentation:

Have you ever wondered who God loves the most? All of us have been given different and unique gifts and abilities. It is easy to think that the gift you have been given is not as important as somebody else's gift. Or, maybe you think that your ability makes you better. In Luke 9:46 the disciples began to wonder which one of them was the greatest- who did God think was the best?

Take a look at these three ropes (Figure #1). I am going to tie them into circles, representing the circles we often find ourselves in. We often have a circle of friends at school (tie the red end of one rope to the red end of another - Figure #2). Maybe we have another circle of friends at church (tie the blue ends together). It is easy to surround ourselves with people who are like us or maybe just people that we like. We can even begin to feel that people who are not in our circle (tie the yellow ends together), or people who do not have the same gifts we do, are simply not as good or important as we are (Figure #3).

The reality is that we are all different, but that does not mean that we can just form our own little circle because we do not need anyone else. In 1 Corinthians 12 we are told that, as Christians, even though there are many parts, we are all one body. In fact, verse 25 says that there should be no division in the body, but that its parts should have equal concern for each other. In other words, instead of separating ourselves, we need to all (toss all three circles into the air, allowing them to come down as one large circle - Figure #4) work together!

Helpful Hints:

You can change the length of the ropes to make it easier for your hands to hold and tie. Do practice tying all of the ropes and keeping them in your hand. Try laying the circle over the back of your hand after you tie it to make it easier to tie the next circle.

Chapter Twenty-Four
Shielded By Faith

The Whole Armor of God

Verse: Ephesians 6:10-17 (NIV)
Finally, be strong in the Lord and in His mighty power.
Put on the full armor of God so that you can take your stand
against the devil's schemes. For our struggle is not against flesh
and blood, but against the rulers, against the authorities, against
the powers of this dark world and against the spiritual forces of
evil in the heavenly realms. Therefore put on the full armor of
God, so that when the day of evil comes, you may be able to
stand your ground, and after you have done everything, to stand.
Stand firm then, with the belt of truth buckled around your waist,
with the breastplate of righteousness in place, and with your feet
fitted with the readiness that comes from the gospel of peace. In
addition to all this, take up the shield of faith, with which you
can extinguish all the flaming arrows of the evil one. Take the
helmet of salvation and the sword of the Spirit, which is the
word of God.

Materials Needed:
(1) Dollar bill
(1) Sharpened Pencil
(1) Small paper picture representing each part of the whole
    armor of God (the shield should be about 2/3 the size of the
    dollar bill).

Figure #1 - Materials Needed

Concept:

A pencil (representing the flaming arrows of the evil one) is repeatedly shoved through a dollar bill (representing our lives). The audience can clearly hear the paper tearing, yet when the bill is displayed at the end, it is shown to be unharmed.

How to do it:

A small slit is cut in the dollar bill ahead of time. On the face side of the bill, there is a small letter to the left of the face in the center. Cut a straight line from the top to bottom of that letter and the circle surrounding it (Figure #2 and #3). Cutting on the letter will help to conceal the cut.

When the bill is folded, the pencil actually passes through this cut and does not appear to harm the bill. To fold the dollar correctly, begin by folding it in half with the face side in. Then, take the end of the bill on the right side (the opposite side of the letter you previously put the cut in) and fold it back down to the outside. This fold should come right to the letter with the secret cut (Figure #4). When you place the paper shield around the dollar bill and put the pencil through, you simply push the pencil through the secret hole so it does not harm the bill (Figures #5, #6, and #7).

The pencil will push through the paper shield. This allows the audience to see and hear the pencil pass through the paper. They will be even more amazed when you finally remove the pencil and show that although the shield is damaged, the dollar bill is unharmed (Figure #8).

Figure #2

Figure #3

Figure #4

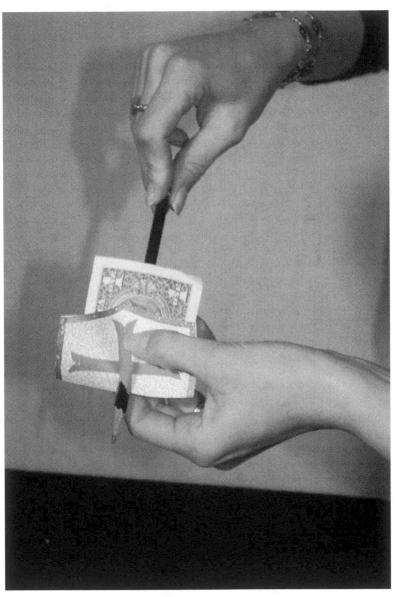

Figure #5

Figure #6

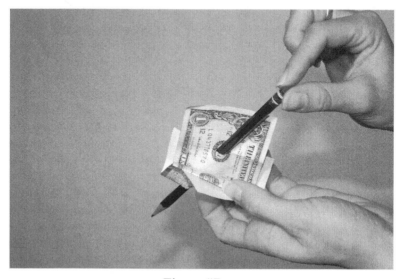

Figure #7

136

Figure #8

Presentation:

Each of us is valuable to God. God has a very special plan and purpose for your life. The reality is as Christians we are in a battle. Now, this is not a physical battle against human beings but a spiritual battle against the evil one. He has plans to attempt to destroy us Christians.

In Ephesians 6:10 Paul teaches us about putting on the armor of God. We must put on the belt of truth, the chest armor of righteousness, shoes of peace, the shield of faith, the helmet of salvation, and the sword of the spirit (when each part of the armor is mentioned hold up the small picture representing that part of the armor, then pick the shield back up, and fold it over the top of the dollar bill - see Figure #1- Materials Needed). There may be times when things come against our life, and the evil one tries to harm us (begin shoving the pencil through the dollar and shield as you talk about the trials we may face - Figures #5 and #6). But, if we have the whole armor of God on, then no matter what comes our way, no matter what kind of persecution we face, what kind of trials there are, or how the evil one tries to tempt us, you will be protected (open the dollar bill back up to reveal it is unharmed - Figure #8) and you can stand firm for Christ!

Helpful Hints:
This works best with a fairly new and crisp dollar bill. A crisp bill will do better at hiding the secret cut. As always, be sure to practice ahead of time. Make sure the cut you put in the bill is wide enough that the pencil does not tear the bill when it passes through, but not too wide that it is obvious. Also, be sure the fold on the right side of the bill lines up with the cut to further cover the pencil going through. When you finish, pull the bill fairly tightly, so the audience cannot see the cut.

Chapter Twenty-Five
The Healer

In our lives other people will sometimes hurt us with the words they say, but Jesus can pick up the pieces and heal our brokenness.

Verse: Psalm 34:17-19 (New Living Translation)
The Lord hears his people when they call to him for help. He rescues them from all their troubles. The Lord is close to the brokenhearted; he rescues those whose spirits are crushed. The righteous person faces many troubles, but the Lord comes to the rescue each time.

Materials Needed:
(1) Handkerchief
(2) Large Wooden Matches
Scissors or utility knife

Concept:
A wooden match is wrapped inside a handkerchief. A volunteer can feel the match as it is broken, but when the handkerchief is opened the match is shown to be restored.

How to do it:
Prepare the handkerchief by cutting a small opening in the outside seam (Figure #1). Hide a duplicate match inside this seam (Figure #2). When the handkerchief is folded up, it is this duplicate match that is actually broken.

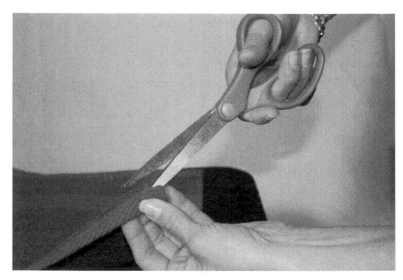

Figure #1

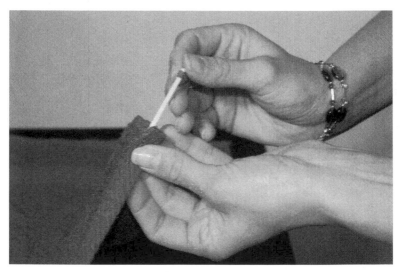

Figure #2

Presentation:

Has anyone ever hurt your feelings? Maybe someone has said or done some things to you that have left you feeling broken. I know this has happened to me. There may have even been times where it was not a matter of people intentionally hurting you, but possibly something sad happened in your life that left you feeling broken hearted. What do we do in times like these?

Take a look at this wooden match. Right now, it is solid. It is intact. This is how we want our lives to be. Nice and solid, everything put together and in order the way it should be. But, then something bad might happen (wrap the match inside of the handkerchief - Figures #3 and #4). It could be something so bad that it makes us feel broken inside (have a volunteer take a hold of the match *inside the hem* and break it. They will think they are breaking the match you just put inside).

God understands that we go through some difficult situations in our life. When we do, we can pray and God will hear us. The Bible tells us in Psalm 34 that the Lord is close to the brokenhearted and rescues those whose spirits are crushed. When we feel broken we can turn to God in prayer and He will rescue us. In fact, He alone can heal our brokenness and even make us stronger (open the handkerchief to reveal the match is restored - Figure #5) than ever before!

141

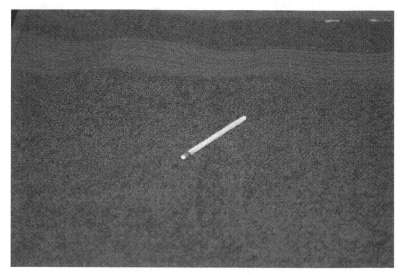

Figure #3

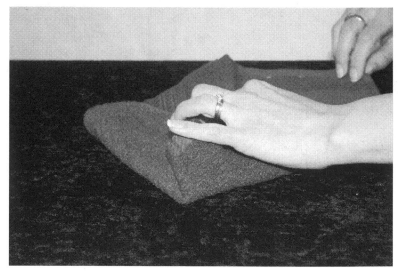

Figure #4

Figure #5

Helpful Hints:

When you begin folding the handkerchief around the match, be careful to keep track of where both matches are (the one the audience has seen and the one in the secret compartment). This way you will be sure to have your volunteer break the correct match!

Chapter Twenty-Six
Here And Gone

We cannot even know what life will be like tomorrow, so be sure to live life to its fullest today.

Verse: James 4:14 (New American Standard Bible)
Yet you do not know what your life will be like tomorrow. You are just a vapor that appears for a little while and then vanishes away.

Materials Needed:
(1) Small drinking glass
Several napkins or paper towels
(1) Table
(1) Quarter or other coin

Concept:
A solid drinking glass is displayed on top of a table. After being covered with napkins, the glass is apparently flattened and then shown to have completely vanished!

How to do it:
The key to this trick is a little misdirection (Figure #3). At first your audience will think you are trying to make the quarter vanish. You do this by placing a glass over the quarter, rim side down. The quarter is now securely contained inside the glass. Paper napkins are now used to cover up the glass. At first, you tap the top of the glass, saying that as this happens, the quarter will disappear.

When the glass is lifted, the quarter is still there. Repeat this again with the quarter a bit closer to the edge of the table. This time, when you lift the glass to see if the quarter has vanished, bring the covered glass over your lap. Your audience will be focused on the quarter to see if it has vanished. While they are looking at the quarter, secretly drop the glass into your lap. Make sure to keep holding the napkins so they retain the form of the glass.

Now, place the napkins over the quarter once again. It will appear that the glass is still there. Smash the napkins flat against the table, and the glass has disappeared!

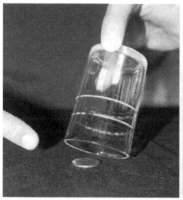

Figure #1

Figure #2

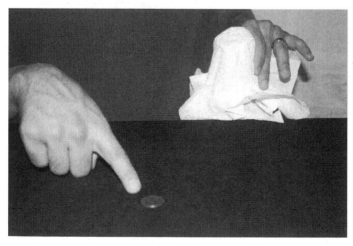

Figure #3

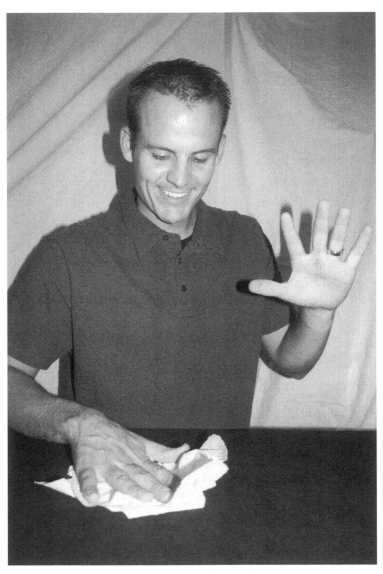

Figure #4

Presentation:

Life can be so full of distractions! It is very easy for us to become consumed with the things of this world that really don't matter, instead of being focused on Jesus and living our lives to fully please Him. This quarter is going to represent those things that often distract us (place the quarter down on the table in front of you). There are times when we may try to capture (place the glass over the quarter - Figure #1) things like money, games, toys, and other things. Although these material things are not necessarily bad, they should never become what is most important to us.

Today, I'm going to try to make this quarter disappear (begin covering the glass with the napkins - Figure #2). Now, you know that even though I have covered up the glass and the quarter below it, the quarter is still there. Let's see if we can get rid of that quarter-those "distractions". We do it, with a little tap (tap the glass through the napkins, then pull the napkins and glass away - Figure #3), and now the quarter has disappeared! Oh, I guess it did not work that time. Sometimes we need to keep trying to get our focus right and get rid of those distractions. Let's try that again. (Move the quarter closer to the edge of the table in preparation for later dropping the glass in your lap). This time, when we tap the glass, the quarter will disappear (tap the glass again, and then pick up the napkin and glass. While the spectators are focused on the quarter, drop the glass into your lap). This is getting a little bit frustrating, but we will try one last time (move the quarter to another spot further away from you. This time, instead of just tapping the glass, flatten the napkin completely against the table - see Figure #4). Wow! I guess the quarter is still there- but the glass is gone!

This can remind us that even in our lives, the unexpected can happen. James 4:14 says that our lives are like a vapor that appears for a little while and then vanish away. We never can be sure what will happen tomorrow, so be sure you are focused on what is most important today- that, of course, is Jesus!

Helpful Hints:

Be sure to use enough napkins to completely cover the glass. Hold the napkins tightly to the glass at first to get them into the form of the glass.

Although this works great when seated at a table, you can also do it while standing. Just make sure that the table or podium you are standing behind has a pillow or blanket on the floor behind it to catch the glass when it falls.

Chapter Twenty-Seven
How "Sweet" It Is!

The greatest treasure in life is only found when we choose to live our life for Jesus Christ.

Verse: Matthew 13:44 (New Living Translation)
The Kingdom of Heaven is like a treasure that a man discovered hidden in a field. In his excitement, he hid it again and sold everything he owned to get enough money to buy the field.

Materials Needed:
(1) Dollar bill
(1) Marker
(5) Small sugar packets

Concept:
A dollar bill, representing a person's life, is marked by a volunteer and then vanishes. It later reappears inside a sugar packet chosen freely by the volunteer.

How to do it:
After your volunteer marks the dollar bill, fold it up into a small packet (small enough to hide behind one of the sugar packets - Figure #1 and #2). Hold the packet between the fingers and thumb of your left hand with your palm facing up (Figure #3). As your right hand comes over the top of the bill to pick it up, secretly drop the bill into the palm of your left hand (Figures #4 and #5). Raise your right hand up, keeping it closed, as if you now have the bill in that hand (at this point it is really in your left - Figure #6). Lifting your right hand in the air will direct the

audience's attention to this hand and take the focus away from your left hand.

Have your volunteer select a sugar packet. Pick the sugar up with your left hand, and allow it to cover the dollar bill still hidden there (Figure #7). When the packet of sugar is opened, simply drop the dollar bill out from behind the packet as the sugar pours onto the table.

Figure #1

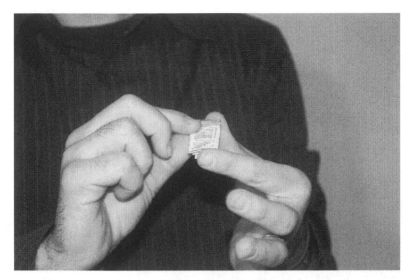

Figure #2

Figure #3

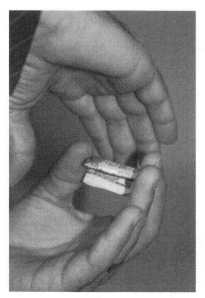

Figure #4

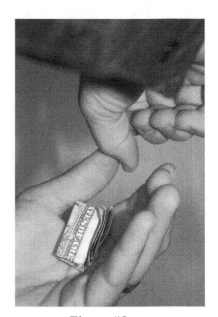

Figure #5

154

Figure #6

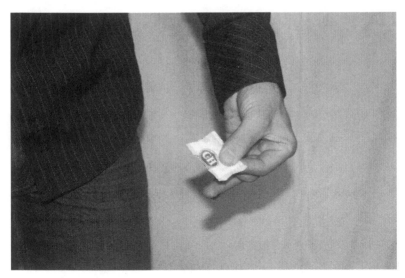

Figure #7

Figure #8

Figure #9

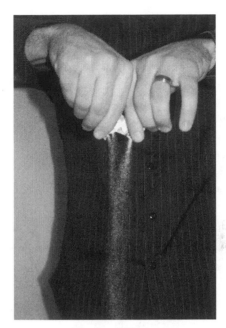

Figure #10

Figure #11

Figure #12

Figure #13

Presentation:

In the Bible there is a story in which Jesus says that Heaven is like a treasure that a man found in a field. He was so excited about this treasure that he buried it. He then went and sold everything he owned, so he would have the money to buy the field where the treasure was buried.

If we knew for sure what kind of treasure we were getting in return, a lot of our decisions would be much easier. But, are we really willing to give up everything to follow God? Today I'm going to need a volunteer to help me (bring your volunteer up from the audience). I am so thankful that you are here to help me that I would like to pay you, is that okay? I want you to have this dollar. This is your dollar and nobody else's, so what I want you to do is take this marker and write your name, draw a picture, or put your initials on the bill. Mark on it in some specific way so that if you were to lose it and somebody else found it, we would all know for sure that this dollar bill belonged to you (hold the bill up so your audience can see it has been marked - Figure #1).

Now, you have an important decision. This dollar bill is going to represent your life. Of course, your life is worth far more than just a dollar. I could never give you enough money to tell you what your life is worth. In fact, your life is a treasure. Each of us wants to do everything we can to hold tightly to that treasure. But, we all have a choice. Today we are going to find out if there is a better treasure out there for you.

There are five packets of sugar here, and I would like you to choose one of them (have the volunteer select a sugar packet and give it to you - Figure #7). This packet of sugar may at first seem rather worthless, but today it is going to stand for something very important. This sugar packet is going represent God's plan for your life. It is pretty "sweet"! Today you have a choice. Remember, the dollar bill in my hand represents your life, and the sugar packet represents God's plan for your life. Each of us can choose to do our own thing and live life our own way, or we can choose to follow God's plan for our life. Today I am going to give you the choice; do you want to keep your dollar bill, or would you like to trade it for God's plan for your life (Figure #8)? (If the volunteer says they want to make the trade, simply say "I think that is a great decision", and open your hand to show the dollar bill has vanished. If the volunteer wants to keep their dollar, simply say "some people do make that decision, but in the end if we choose to follow our own plan, our life is not worth much." Then open your hand to show the bill has vanished - Figure #9).

If we try to live life for ourselves and do things our own way, in the end we will lose! There is really no value in living life for our own selfish purposes. We can try to hold on to what we think is a treasure, but the real treasure can only be found in Jesus Christ (now display the selected sugar packet. As you rip it open and the sugar falls to the table, allow the dollar bill to drop onto the table as well - see Figures #10 and #11). Take a close look at that dollar bill. In fact, pick it up and open it up (Figures #12 and #13). If you look closely you will notice that this is the same dollar bill you just marked a moment ago!

The truth is that if we are willing to give up everything to follow Jesus, in the end we do not lose anything. We gain more than we ever could have imagined!

Helpful Hints:

Put some time into practicing the move in which you pretend to pick the dollar up in your right hand and steal it away with your left (Figures #3, #4, and #5). The tendency is to hold your left hand up. You want to try and relax your left hand as much as possible, and let it hang down by your side. This will probably feel a bit awkward at first, and you will be a bit self-conscious about this hand.

Practice until you can do this with confidence. Also, hold your right hand up in the air as if you are truly holding something (Figure #6). This will help draw the attention of your audience to your right hand.

Chapter Twenty-Eight
NUTS!

We often think we know what is best, but we should never decide we know more than God.

Verse: Proverbs 3:5-6 (NIV)
Trust in the Lord with all your heart and lean not on your own understanding; in all your ways acknowledge him, and he will make your paths straight.

Materials Needed:
(3) Empty nut cans
(1) Matchbox
(1) Rubber band
A few coins or nuts to place inside the matchbox.

Concept:
Three cans of nuts are displayed. Two are empty and one apparently still has some nuts inside. The cans are "shuffled" around the table while the audience tries to keep their eyes on the can with the nuts. At any time you can make each

can appear to be either empty or full. Finally, all three cans are opened to reveal they were empty all along.

How to do it:

All three cans are empty the entire time. The secret is that you have a matchbox under your sleeve which has been rubber banded to your wrist (Figure 1). Inside the matchbox are a few coins or some nuts (Figure 2). When you pick up a can with this hand and shake it, the nuts in the matchbox will make a noise and make your audience think that can has nuts in it.

Figure 1   Figure 2

Presentation:

Today I have a test for you. There are three cans here that use to be full of nuts. Two are now empty (hold up and shake two cans to show they are empty). It is up to you to keep track of where the nuts are (shake the third can, and the matchbox with the nuts attached to your wrist, so the audience thinks they hear the nuts inside). To start, I'll try and make it easy on you. Watch closely (mix up the cans fairly slowly, and pay attention to which can you showed to have the nuts in it). Now, which can has the nuts inside? Is the one on my left, the one in the middle or the one on the right? (Show the first two cans empty, and pick up the same can as before and shake it to show that it seems to be full) Good!

Let's try that again (mix the cans up a bit faster, again letting the audience guess correctly). Now, which one has the nuts? Nice job! I can tell it will be difficult for me to fool a smart audience like you, but let me try this a bit faster this time (mix the cans up even faster and for a longer period this time). Did you keep up that time? Who thinks it is in this can (point to the can, then pick it up and shake it to show it is empty)? Not quite, how about this one (This should be the can your originally showed to have the nuts, but now it will appear to be empty. Do not pick it up and shake it yet, just point to it)? Would you be willing to trust me if I told you they were not in that can? Some of you say yes, and it sounds like some of you would rather trust in your own eyes. Let's see (pick it up and shake it to demonstrate it to be empty) - no not that can either.

This time it is this can here (pick up the last can and shake it so they hear the nuts)! Watch again (mix the cans up one last time). Are you confused yet, or are you with me? Let's take a vote. Raise your hand if you think the nuts are here in this can (this time shake the can and then open it and show the audience it is empty). No, that was not it. Raise your hand if you think they are in this can (again, just point to it. Do not open it yet). One more time, who would be willing to trust me if I told you they were not in that can either? The rest of you would still rather trust your own understanding I see. Let's check (shake the can and remove the lid to show the audience it is empty as well), they were not in that one either.

Let's make it easier- raise your hand if you think the nuts are in this can. Actually (open the final can and show it to also be empty), if you thought any of these cans had nuts in them than you are the one who is NUTS (Figure 3)!

Figure 3

That may be confusing. In fact, for some of you it was confusing enough that you were willing to trust me and not your own eyes. Others were so sure they knew which can was correct that they were not willing to trust me even when I gave you a second chance. That's ok for this little test, because it is just a trick. But, in life, there are times where God may ask us to trust in Him even though it does not make sense to us.

Our understanding may make us think that we know what is best. We may not be willing to give or share because we think we will be better off if we keep things to ourselves. We may be tempted to steal because we think we will then have more and be happier. We may even be tempted to give into temptation and do things we know God does not want us to do because it seems to us our friends, or people we want to be our friends, will like us more if we do!

No matter what the circumstance, in all things we need to trust the Lord and follow Him. Proverbs 3:5-6 gives us a perfect reminder of this when it says to trust in the Lord with all your heart and lean not on your own understanding. In all your ways acknowledge Him and He will make your paths straight! In all you do today and everyday, trust in the Lord and keep Him number one in your life!

Helpful Hints:

It is a good idea to let the audience guess correctly which can has the nuts in it the first few times. This then really throws them off when later they are incorrect. Also, practice ahead of time to see how much you can move without the nuts in the matchbox making noise and how much you do need to move to create the appropriate sound.

Chapter Twenty-Nine
Restored

We have been separated by God because of our sin, but we can be restored to a relationship with Him through Jesus Christ.

Verse: Romans 6:23 (New Living Translation)
For the wages of sin is death, but the free gift of God is eternal life through Christ Jesus our Lord.

Materials Needed:
(1) Piece of Rope (approximately four feet in length)
Scissors

Concept:

   A rope is seemingly cut in half, and then tied together. The knot connecting the ropes is then removed to show that the rope is truly restored.

How to do it:

   The rope is actually not cut in half. Rather, the rope is cut about three or four inches from one end. Hold the ends of the rope in your left hand with the center of the rope hanging down in a loop. As you grab the middle of the loop and bring it up by the ends (Figure 1), secretly leave the center behind the palm of your hand, and pull up the area three or four inches from either end (Figure 2). When you cut this small piece, it will appear to your audience that you cut the rope in half (Figure 3).

   This small piece is then tied over the center of the longer rope (Figure 4). Because at this point it is really just a small piece of rope tied over a longer piece, you can simply grab the small piece and slide it toward either end (Figure 5). Finally, the piece is completely removed from the rope to show the complete restoration (Figure 6).

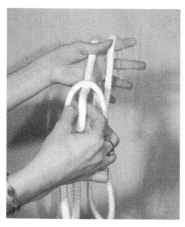
Figure 1

Figure 2

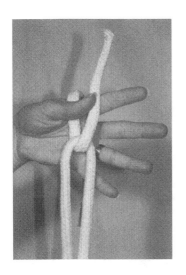

Figure 3

This is the back view (what you will see). From the audience perspective your hand will cover the loop and create the illusion that the rope has been cut in half.

Figure 4

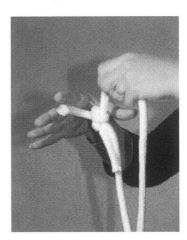

Figure 5

Figure 6

Presentation:

Each and every one of us was created by God. When God made us, it was His plan for us to have a solid and unbroken relationship with him (as you say this, pull tightly on the rope to illustrate that it is solid). But, there is a problem. The problem is that all of us have sinned (bring the center of the rope up in your hands, switching it for a piece near the end as in the illustration, cut the rope near the end). Because of that sin we have been completely separated from God.

The Bible also tells us that the wages of sin is death. We may ask the question "What can I do to mend that relationship back together so I can be with God?" Some people might say that you need to do good works and be a good person. Others might say that you just need to go to church enough times (as you give these and other examples of what people might think they can do to restore their relationship with God, tie the small piece of rope over the larger one). As you can see, those things are "not" the way. Just like this rope is really "not" put back together.

It is only through Jesus Christ who came to this world and lived a perfect life for me and for you. He then paid the penalty for our sins when He died on the cross. But Jesus did not stay dead. He rose from the grave! It is only by accepting Jesus Christ as your personal Lord and Savior that you can truly be forgiven.

Only Jesus can forgive you and completely take away that sin in your life (slide the knot off the end of the rope illustrating Jesus taking away our sin). Then and only then can you be reconnected with God and experience that strong and unbroken relationship with him!

Helpful Hints:

Practice several times bringing the center section of the rope up and switching it out for the smaller piece near the end. Experiment with how you hold the rope, so you can discover what works best for you to do this smoothly. When it comes time to cut the rope, be sure to double check yourself, and cut in the right place.

Chapter Thirty
Knot Possible!

God is able to help us accomplish the things that we may have thought were impossible.

Verse: Philippians 4:13 (New Living Translation)
For I can do everything through Christ, who gives me strength.

Materials Needed:
(2) Equal length pieces of rope (approximate five feet)

Concept:
The performer demonstrates the ability to tie a knot in a rope without letting go of the ends. When a volunteer attempts to do the same thing, it seems to be impossible. Even when the volunteer follows the exact same steps as the performer, the volunteer is still unable to tie a knot without letting go of the ends.

How to do it:

This too is just an illusion. Although it appears that you never let go of the ends of the rope, there is one point in which you do change your grip on the rope. Begin by holding one end of the rope in each of your hands (Figure #1). Next, bring the rope that is in your right hand over the top of your left wrist and down (the motion of your right hand begins close to your body and moves away from your body and over the wrist - Figures #2 and #3) . This should create a loop hanging from your left wrist with the end of the rope hanging down behind it (Figure #4).

Now, reach through the loop with your right hand and with the back of your hand pull the length of rope hanging down behind back through the loop (Figures #5, #6, and #7). Have your volunteer follow along the best they can (Figure #8). This can be a lot of fun! Finally, turn your hands palms down and then "throw" the rope forward off of your wrist. This is where the real trick takes place. As you turn your wrists so your palms are facing down let go of the rope in your right hand with your four fingers, maintaining a grip only with your thumb (Figure #9). This will bring a different section of rope right into the palm of your right hand. As the rope is tossed forward, simply grab onto this other section of rope with the four fingers of your right hand while letting go of the section you were holding with your thumb (Figures #10 and #11). A knot is now created (Figure #12) - impossible!

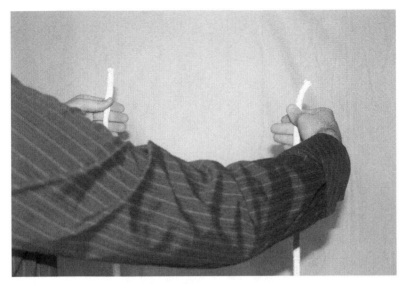

Figure #1

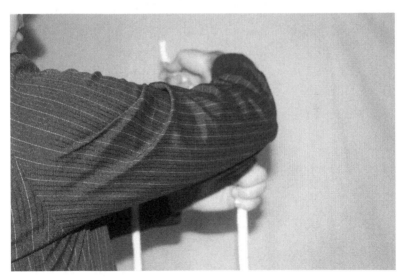

Figure #2

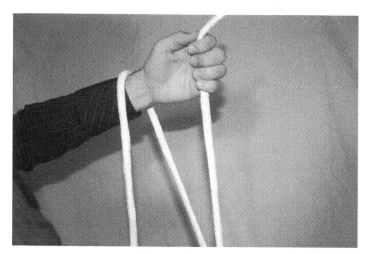

Figure #3

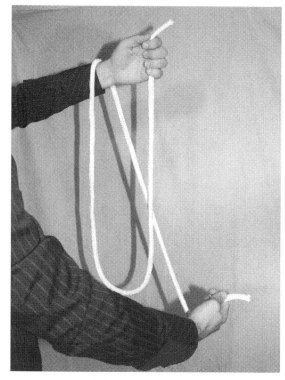

Figure #4

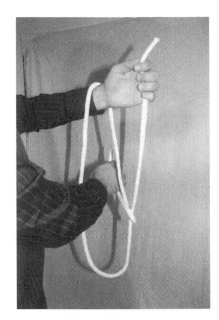

Figure #5

Figure #6

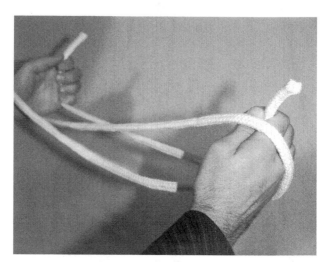

Figure #7

Figure #8
180

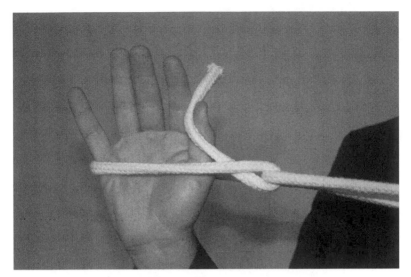

Figure #9

Figure #10

Figure #11

Figure #12

Presentation:

It has often been said that it is impossible to tie a knot in a rope without letting go of the ends. Let's take a quick survey. How many of you think it is possible to tie a knot in a rope without letting go? How many think it is impossible?

I'm going to have a volunteer help me with this and see if we can do it (bring your volunteer up and have them try to tie a knot without letting go). I don't know if it is impossible, but it definitely looks difficult. The same could be said about a lot of things in life. There are many things that seem extremely difficult if not completely impossible. Maybe you have even felt that there is something God wants you to do with your life, but you feel it is impossible. Like tying a knot without letting go.

Some people have given up on hopes and dreams that God has placed in their heart because people told them it was impossible. We always need to remember that even though people might tell you it cannot happen (begin tying your knot as in the instructed way); with God nothing is impossible (show the knot tied in the rope)!

Helpful Hints:

This sounds a lot more complicated than it is- so try it! You will have a ton of fun with this. Because the rope is not gimmicked in any way, you can use any rope that is long enough and even trade back and forth with your volunteer to add to the fun.

Bonus Idea:

After tying a knot "without letting go" it is a lot of fun to go back through the process with your volunteer still in place. The volunteer can watch you tie your knot and even follow the process step by step. As long as the volunteer does not know to reposition their hand over the different section of rope (as described previously), when they toss their rope forward at the end it will not have a knot in it. This can further illustrate the fact that a trick only works when you know the secret of how to do it. For us, there is no more secret- if we follow God's plan and will for our lives than nothing is impossible with Him!

About David and Teesha

David and Teesha Laflin are illusionists with a passion for ministry. Thousands of people have been impacted by their unique and creative way of presenting the life-changing message of Jesus Christ through illusions and creative object lessons.

Their presentations have served churches and other ministries all across the United States and around the world. In fact, two months of outreach programs in India was the beginning of their full-time ministry. It was here that they truly discovered how effective the art of illusion can be in presenting the gospel. In other countries, including the Dominican Republic, Venezuela, Romania, Bolivia, Rwanda, and more they have taught native missionaries how to use creative teaching tools like illusions for effective evangelism.

David and Teesha's high-energy, fast-paced, colorful programs have also been featured on Daystar Christian Television and by many of the nation's leading Christian conferences and conventions. David and Teesha have also made hundreds of live appearances at churches, outreach events, schools, and corporations.

To find out more about David and Teesha Laflin, visit:
www.davidandteesha.com